Succes___ _____ !

Conceive. Believe. Achieve.

THE
female
EDGE

Norsemen Books

Sybil

SYBIL VERCH

☆ Author's Proof — Ignore Typos ☺

Print Edition ISBN: 978-1-988172-24-8

eBook Edition ISBN: 978-1-988172-25-5

Printed in the United States of America

Published by Norsemen Books™

ATTENTION CORPORATIONS, UNIVERSITIES, COLLEGES AND PROFESSIONAL ORGANIZATIONS: Quantity discounts are available on bulk purchases of this book for educational, gift purposes, or as premiums for increasing memberships. Special book covers or book excerpts can be created to fit specific needs. For more information, please contact Norsemen Books: info@norsemenbooks.com or www.sybilverch.com.

Dedication

To my amazing husband, Chad Verch, for your

ongoing support and encouragement.

You continuously inspire me to be a better person.

CONTENTS

PREFACE

You are a woman in a male-dominated society. Get over it.

Yes, sometimes we get treated unfairly and sometimes we get harassed, talked over, bullied, stereotyped and left out. But guess what? We have more control over how we are treated, and more power to direct how we are treated, than we give ourselves credit for. I'm not saying it's okay or that we are responsible for it. It is most definitely not okay and we are most definitely not responsible for it. But I am suggesting there is a way we can change the outcome.

I changed my outcome by not accepting the limiting messages I was given at the outset of my career. When I started in the finance industry, I was told I would fail as an advisor because I was young, female, and pretty. The firm didn't want to hire me, but I leveraged their need for my administrative skills to open a new office and to negotiate a position as an advisor once I was done. I proved them wrong because I demonstrated success in gathering assets, building client relationships and generating profit for the firm.

I would love to be writing this book in an era when we are no longer talking about gender equality or diversity issues in our culture and our workplaces. That would mean we have achieved true equality, diversity and equal opportunity for all.

But we haven't. Yet.

In writing this book my intention is to focus on strengthening the female voice and sharing with women what we can do to create more opportunities for ourselves both in the workplace and in our lives.

As a woman who has worked damn hard for the success I enjoy—in a field I was told I had no place in—I have learned a lot about getting ahead in an authentic way.

I have learned what it takes and what the secret obstacle actually is. (Spoiler alert: it's us.)

I want to share my story and wisdom with women who are ready to step up in their lives to achieve what they really want, whatever that may be.

In writing this book and interviewing both men and women, it has become apparent that some men are now feeling left out. What a great irony! The 'Old Boys Club' is slowly dying and some of its members are having a hard time coping.

In addition, younger men don't fully understand the issues women faced and the challenges we have overcome to ensure equality. They are asking, 'What about me?' They're finding out that many Fortune 500 companies are pushing for gender equality and offering special training programs to help women step up to the plate. This is off-putting for men, both old school and new. Having enjoyed the easy ride for so long, they now feel marginalized—something women have experienced from Day One.

Ladies, we can't afford to lose time or momentum appeasing their egos. For too many years men have enjoyed a business culture where deals get done at the expense of women.

 Women are rising, companies are noticing, and markets are applauding.

Academic research bears out why companies are taking note. In a 2011 paper published in *Harvard Business Review*, authors Anita Wooley and Thomas Malone found that there's little correlation between a group's collective intelligence and the IQs of its individual members. But if a group includes more women, its collective intelligence rises[1]. The conventional argument is that diversity is good and you should have both men and women in a group. But the data shows the more women the better. Many studies have shown that women tend to score higher on tests of social sensitivity than men do. What is really important is to have people who are high in social sensitivity, whether they are men or women.

The definition of 'group' includes the C-suite. In a 2016 Harvard Business School paper studying profitable firms, Marcus Noland and Tyler Moran[2] associated firms with at least 30% women in corporate leadership roles (CEO, the board and other C-suite positions) with a one-percentage-point increase in net margin—which translates to a 15% increase in profitability for a typical firm.

If you're choosing industries, Noland and Moran also note that financial services, health care, utilities and telecommunications are relatively welcoming to female leadership while fewer women were found at the top in basic materials, technology, energy and industrial sectors.

We can all agree that we want the best person for the job, but unconscious biases are still getting in the way of tapping into the best talent available. By pushing for gender diversity on boards and at the senior executive level, it creates a win-win for everyone. It's definitely good for the economy, the business, the team, and in the end, the individual. Everyone wins when we level the playing field.

---

[1] https://hbr.org/2011/06/defend-your-research-what-makes-a-team-smarter-more-women
[2] https://hbr.org/2016/02/study-firms-with-more-women-in-the-c-suite-are-more-profitable

I hope many men read this book because this is not about giving more opportunities to women at the expense of men. This is about creating more opportunities for equality, regardless of gender.

Here's the short story:

Ladies: don't blame men or patriarchy any longer. Take ownership of your life. Take the initiative to get what you want out of life. If you don't know how to achieve this and need guidance or inspiration, read on.

Gentlemen: stop complaining that the women are getting more attention in business. You had a long history with an unfair advantage. Embrace these changes and make the most out of living a well-balanced life. If you don't know how to achieve this and need some guidance/inspiration, read on. We'll all be better for it.

"An average person with average talents and ambition and average education, can outstrip the most brilliant genius in our society if that person has clear, focused goals."

Mary Kay Ash

MY EARLY YEARS

I was a tomboy growing up. I liked getting my hands dirty and trying new things. Mom would try to get me to put on a dress for special occasions, but I was determined to wear pants. I had a fairly traditional upbringing. Mom took some time off work when my sister and I were born, then went back to nursing to help support the family. Dad worked full time for an advertising agency while Mom worked evening shifts to eliminate the need for daycare. Their division of household labour was typical: she did most of the cooking, cleaning, and domestic duties while Dad took care of the yard work, repairs, and the handyman tasks that needed attention.

This worked really well as they both seemed to enjoy their roles in an equitable partnership. Mom is a natural nurturer and she is happy when she is helping others. Nursing was a perfect career path for her. She could earn a living doing what she enjoyed and was naturally good at. If money was no object, she likely would have stayed at home to raise the kids, yet I believe it was a good thing that she didn't. The income she earned contributed to their ability to buy a house and send my sister and I to dance lessons. I believe it gave her a sense of purpose and boosted her self-esteem. She never had big aspirations and preferred to take the slow and steady route. That being said, family was her number one priority and still is.

Dad was more of a dreamer and he would often share great ideas for new business opportunities. I remember him talking about opening a photo booth in downtown Victoria during the tourist season for people to get their pictures taken and sent back to their friends and family. This was just as the technology was coming out, before anyone had iPhones to do it themselves. He worked in the advertising industry, and creativity came naturally to him, yet he didn't take the risk to try the great ideas he had. Mom was definitely more conservative and risk averse, so I'm not sure she would have supported any of his wild and crazy ideas.

Both my parents worked outside the home while I was growing up and that seemed normal to me. They set an example of how working hard could generate the income they needed to buy the things they needed and wanted.

I took an interest in both cooking and fixing things. Why couldn't I do both? Having two daughters and no sons, Dad would get us involved in activities that are traditionally thought of as 'boy' activities. That included things like sports and woodworking. The fact that Dad would do things with me that typical dads did with their sons, contributed to my belief that I could do anything I put my mind to. I didn't grasp the idea that pink was for girls, blue was for boys. Society doesn't fully realize how our unconscious biases can have a negative impact in our lives. I was fortunate to have the upbringing I had.

We didn't have much money growing up, but we had everything we needed. I felt unconditional love and support from my parents and I believe it helped me feel secure and built my confidence. My parents both came from modest, hardworking families. Dad grew up in the city of Edmonton, in a family where money was tight. He was one of seven kids and remembers his mom having to add 6 cans of water to one can of soup to make it go farther. To save money, they decided to move from Edmonton to the town of Westlock for Dad's Grade 12 year. Can you imagine being 17 and moving from the big city to a town with a population of 2500? It all worked out though, because it was there that he met Mom.

My parents always did everything they could within a tight budget to put the kids first. We always had a roof over our heads and food on the table, but we didn't have extra money for name-brand clothes or fancy trips. Our family vacations were usually spent camping. It may not have been glamorous, but I had the time of my life and memories to last forever.

When I was about ten years old, we headed to Cowichan Lake for a week to camp with another family. The weather was perfect, but what really excited me was the fun in creating a home away from home. We set up an outdoor kitchen using an old door as a counter. We had a bin as a sink to wash dishes, a Coleman stove to cook on and a cooler as our fridge. We hung tarps to ensure we'd stay dry and covered if it rained. We went fishing in the lake and drank water from the river.

Dad had this great idea to make slingshots. We spent a whole day searching for just the right piece of wood with a perfect fork shape. We scraped off the bark to make it as smooth as possible. We went into the town's thrift store and bought a pair of suede boots and cut the suede to make a pouch for the sling. A piece of rubber surgical tubing was the final piece needed to bring it all together. We set up some tin cans and had target practice. It was an all-day affair followed by an evening of lying on the beach looking for shooting stars to wish upon. If I close my eyes, I can still feel the glow of happiness I experienced that day.

 *The lesson? Money does not buy happiness. Most of the best things in life are free.*

Have you ever had that feeling of bliss? A moment when everything just feels right? That's the feeling I'm talking about. You can't pay money to get it, it has to come from within.

We moved from Edmonton to Victoria in 1978 because there was a good job opportunity for Dad. In those days it was cheaper to live in Victoria than Edmonton. Now it's the reverse, but that was what opened the door for them. They bought their first house when I was five. I still remember how exciting it was! I asked Mom how much it cost, and she simply answered 'a lot '. I asked where they got the money for it and she explained they took out a mortgage. And there I was, age five, learning what a mortgage was. I was interested in money and finance from that day onwards.

The house was located in a lower income area, but it was a first step in building equity. They didn't feel that the other families in the neighborhood were good role models for us, but it was what they could afford at the time.

I was a kid on the go who got involved in everything.

Many kids in the neighborhood tended to get into trouble, stealing and other activities they shouldn't be doing. As soon as my parents could afford to move, we moved to a nicer area.

I've always been very independent and as a result often challenged people's thinking. I asked a lot of questions—what, why, how, when, who—and I was good at figuring out how to get what I want. I'm sure I wore out my parents.

I liked to be busy and I wanted to join everything. I was in several dance classes (ballet, tap and jazz), the school sports teams, the school band and the student council. Mom was concerned about me doing too much and suggested I say no to something. I convinced her that I could handle it. I had thought through my schedule and talked her through my plan so she could see how I would fit everything in. She asked how I would fit in homework and I said I would do it right after school before my scheduled activities started. I had an answer for everything she asked. It made me happy to do all those things. She agreed. I kept my word, maintained my grades and continued to keep a smile on my face.

I look at my son today who has similar traits. He pushes back. He challenges me. He's very good at getting what he wants. When Otis, our black lab died, Levi was thirteen and desperately wanted to get another dog. I wasn't so keen. I had a busy work and travel schedule and didn't see how having another dog would fit in our busy lifestyle.

When I tried to explain that having a dog is expensive, he offered to chip in his own money.

When I explained that his dad and I plan to do even more travelling once he's in university and didn't want to be tied down with a dog, he said he would take care of the dog. He even talked his grandparents into taking the dog on a part-time basis.

When I said having a dog is a lot of work and they need regular exercise, he said 'Mom, picture this . . . you can be sitting on the back patio of our new house (which we were in the process of building) in the summer with a drink in one hand and a ball thrower in the other. You can be enjoying the sun and the view without even having to get up.' I broke out in laughter as he was really trying to paint me a picture of how great an experience it would be.

He researched various breeds and chose a French bulldog as they don't need much exercise, are small and therefore easy to take places, and are very affectionate. I finally caved in and am now the proud owner of a French bulldog named Rudy. I must admit it is great having him as part of the family.

As a parent, I now know how challenging this is. Exasperated, I will find myself sometimes saying to my son, 'Just do what I tell you to do!' and realize how similar we are. Now I try to really appreciate his assertive independence and recognize that I don't want him to do what everybody tells him to do without ever questioning the rightness of it, even when it's me.

I want him to think for himself. I want him to be empowered to ask all the questions I was free to pose when I was growing up and still ask today. Especially, 'Why?' and, 'Does this make sense?'

Try to create win-win scenarios. Be very thoughtful of how actions impact others. And if you can work in a way to get what you want, it's a benefit to all parties.

As a young girl, fantasizing about my future, I knew I wanted to be a business owner and to make a good income. I wanted to marry a man who was very supportive and would share responsibility for domestic chores. I challenged what was considered the norm and dug deep to realize what I really wanted, regardless of what others expected or thought was appropriate.

It wasn't a typical path 'for a girl'.

I specifically remember having a conversation with a group of girls who all thought they would marry a man who made a good income so they didn't have to work. They believed their place was to have children and take care of the home. They found it a bit odd that I wanted to pursue a career and to be the breadwinner.

I remember thinking to myself, why can't I do anything I want? Why should I limit myself to what is expected and accepted? Societal norms at that time had men working to support the family while women stayed home with the kids and took care of the household. While that works for many, it wasn't what I wanted to do.

Some women love that role and it's right for them. If that's truly what you want, go for it.

I can only assume I was born with a desire to be independent and to challenge the status quo. I rarely take things at face value, and always question things until they make sense to me. Just because something has been done a certain way for so long, doesn't mean it's the right, or the only way. This is the type of critical thinking that helps people succeed in business.

I can't think of any one particular role model in my life that inspired me. I just had this idea about what I wanted to do. I wanted to fix and build things. I look back at what I did for fun as a kid—riding bikes, building dirt jumps, and exploring—and I was drawn to activities that were active, challenging and got my hands and clothes dirty. You couldn't put a dress on me at that stage in my life. I just did what most kids who are raised in healthy environments do: find the fun and throw myself wholeheartedly into it.

I didn't come from a well-educated family with money, but I came from a family that had common sense and a lot of love. I was the first one on either side of the family to get a university degree.

My grandfather was naturally entrepreneurial. He was a farmer and actively volunteered in the community. He was on the board of the seed-cleaning plant in the town of Westlock. The plant was on the verge of bankruptcy when he got involved. He led the charge to save it and helped turn it into a very profitable venture. He only had a grade six education, but problem-solving came naturally to him. His keen common sense enabled him to see what needed to be done and his natural leadership skills empowered him to step up and fix things. The more I learn about my grandfather, the more I understand where I get my business sense from.

I learned that if I wanted something, I could work hard to get it. I didn't have to rely on my parents to buy it for me. I set up lemonade stands and even made things to sell on the sidewalk in front of our house. I remember saving enough money to buy something out of an Avon catalogue and feeling so proud I had earned the money myself. It gave me a sense of independence and I love that feeling! I want every woman to feel that way.

By the time I was eleven, I had a paper route. It wasn't the best job for me since it required waking up at the crack of dawn—I wouldn't call myself a morning person. Either Mom or Dad would get up early too as they didn't want me roaming the neighborhood in the dark by myself. The money wasn't great, but it was a good lesson in discipline, routine, and basic money management.

At fifteen I was working at a ladies clothing store. I was saving money to buy a car when I turned sixteen. At sixteen, I was saving to buy the things I would need when I moved out after high school. I'm not sure what drove me to think ahead like that, but I do like to be prepared and that entails anticipating what comes next.

It feels good to know you can take care of yourself and not be dependent on anyone else—to believe in yourself and anything you put your mind to.

Women who feel good about themselves, who feel strong and independent, are less likely to get themselves in difficult situations. With financial security comes choices, and it's those choices that can make all the difference in life. I was lucky to have had that inner drive for independence at a young age.

I was always a very good student, straight A's or close to, and learning came easily for me. I didn't have to put a lot of effort into it. I was organized and I scheduled time for all the things I wanted to fit in. I would often complete my homework on breaks or right after school so I could have my afternoons, evenings and weekends free to take dance classes, participate in student council meetings, work part time, and spend time with my friends. I felt completely on top of everything in my life and fully in control.

But in Grade 12, I met a boy...

ELIMINATE TOXIC RELATIONSHIPS

A plan usually has a way of coming to fruition, but the path it takes to get there may not always be what you had in mind.

I moved out on my own right after I graduated high school, just as I had planned. But it wasn't because I was ready. I was 17 years old. I needed to move out of the city to get away from an abusive boyfriend.

It was the summer before my grade twelve year when I started dating Tom[3]. Things started off great. Our first couple of months together were fun. He was a bit older than me, good looking and liked to have a good time. We were of the age where going to parties was a regular occurrence and I was enjoying it.

I was attracted to his carefree attitude (which I later discovered was more like laziness) and it made me think that maybe I was pushing myself too hard. I started looking at the choices I made differently.

Then the problems started.

Tom started showing possessive qualities. He tried to dictate what I could wear. He became upset if I wore something he thought was too revealing or something that other guys might find attractive. He wanted to know where I was at all times and didn't approve of me going to social gatherings unless he was there too.

At first I thought he just wanted to be with me all the time so I would

---

3 Tom is obviously a fictitious name

rearrange my plans to spend more time with him. I was obsessed with keeping him happy which led to me skipping school. My grades began to suffer. I didn't care.

My parents didn't like Tom as they could see he was taking me down the wrong path. This created intense friction in the family. The more they tried to push him away, the more I defended him and was determined to prove them wrong.

I had never experienced that type of behaviour. My parents had a healthy, loving and supportive relationship. I kept seeing the good in Tom and thought we would work through it.

I was wrong.

His control issues started impacting my life, and when I would push back he would lose it. He'd punch walls, throw things and yell at me.

I was scared.

After his tantrums, he would apologize and—even worse—cry. He was convincing and I always wound up believing him and giving him another chance.

In the beginning, the abuse was verbal and emotional. Eventually it became physical. He slapped me across the face on one occasion, and kicked me on another.

I still didn't leave.

I remember watching movies about abused women and thinking 'Why don't they just leave?' and 'How stupid to stay'. Yet I had become one of 'those' women.

One evening I had plans with my girlfriend. When she arrived to pick me up, Tom freaked out and said I couldn't go. He threw a clock at the wall and started yelling at me to stay. I was scared and wanted to calm him down, so I assured him I would stay in.

As I was apologizing to my friend for cancelling our plans, she remained calm and supportive. She was my one true friend who stayed by my side and never spoke unkindly of Tom, even though I knew she couldn't stand him. She said to me, 'Sybil, don't worry about what I want or what Tom wants . . . what do *you* want?'

I ran out the door and to her car as fast as I could.

I was terrified of what he would do, but in that moment I broke a little bit of the hold he had on me—not because I defied him, but because I had finally stood up for myself.

Even though it was a turning point, that's still not where the story ends. After a nice evening together, my friend and I arrived back at my place to find Tom waiting for me and lurking in the shadows near a lamppost.

I told him it was over and got into the house as quickly as I could. Thirty minutes later he called me to say he would kill himself and my family if I didn't meet with him.

I should have called 911, but I was young and naïve.

My friend and I drove to meet him at a nearby shopping plaza. I told him again that it was over and he needed to move on, but he became hysterical. We tried to calm him down, but couldn't. He smashed his head through the window of an insurance company and almost sliced his ear right off. The security alarms were going off and he was bleeding badly.

We rushed him to the hospital for medical attention. While he was in with the doctor, I called the police to report the incident anonymously. I wanted to ensure the insurance company was notified, but I didn't want to disclose my name or explain the whole situation. What a mess!

For the next few weeks, Tom went to counseling and tried to change his ways. He begged me to give him another chance and said he'd do anything to make it work.

Stupid me, I believed him and gave him another chance.

I had discovered earlier in our relationship that his dad was abusive to his mom before they got divorced and I even witnessed him getting into a physical fight with his dad. He didn't have the right role models growing up and my heart broke for him because of that. Things were better for the first few weeks, but he started reverting to his old ways.

A few months later, my cousin was visiting from Calgary and met Tom. We all went out for dinner, and afterwards I drove Tom back to his place. I wanted to drop him off and head home to visit with my cousin because she was leaving the next day. He didn't want me to leave and asked me to come in for a bit.

In the hope of avoiding a big scene, I went inside and started making my goodbyes. He started pressing for me to stay overnight. It escalated into an argument and he grabbed me and started yelling.

I knew if I continued to resist, he would become violent. I pretended to give up the fight to defuse the situation. I felt scared, violated and vulnerable.

When he fell asleep—and with tears streaming down my face—I snuck out and ran as fast as I could and drove away.

When I got home, my cousin must have seen that I was upset, but she didn't push to find out why. She simply asked me if I'd like to get away for a while and stay with her in Calgary.

I jumped at the chance.

The following morning I quit my 3 part-time jobs, packed my bags and drove with her. I ran away from everything I knew.

I didn't know how long I would stay, but I got a job after one week and ended up staying for 6 months.

It was one of the best personal growth experiences I have ever had. I felt empowered as I put aside my commitments to others and focused on what I needed for myself.

I learned that I could move cities, find work, make new friends and support myself. I rebuilt my confidence and felt much stronger.

The distance allowed me to look at things from a different perspective. I was now objective. I was no longer in the middle of it. As time went by, I found myself again and started thinking about my future and what I wanted to do next. I gained years of maturity in a matter of months.

I never understood why women in abusive relationships stayed, but inadvertently I had become one. About one third of women around the world experience abuse[4] and I now understand how confusing and disorientating it can be, how messed up your mind can get, and how hard it is to take a step back and

4 www.dvcpartners.org

look at the situation objectively. In a nutshell, I was afraid of the consequences. Ninety-eight percent of women in abusive relationships feel financially tied to their abuser[5] which makes it more difficult to leave and more likely to return.

It took a major incident for me to realize the consequences of staying were far worse than leaving. I was fortunate enough to have a strong support network (many women don't) and the opportunity to leave the city and remove myself from a dangerous situation. It gave me a fresh perspective on life and enabled me to define what was important to me. I became extremely picky when dating other men after that. I vowed to never get myself in a situation like that again.

As I entered the next chapter of my life, I was more confident and knew myself better. The experience taught me to stand up for myself and to distance myself from others who are a negative influence.

 *Whether it's a mean boss, a harassing colleague or an abusive family member, eliminating toxic relationships is key to enjoying life and achieving greater things.*

Putting our own needs first is important, as we are no good to others if we don't take care of ourselves. My business coach says we need to be selflessly selfish, and I agree. That doesn't mean putting yourself first at someone else's expense, it means taking care of yourself so you are in a better position to help others.

---

5 http://nnedv.org/resources

You can't change people—you can only change you. It's not our job to fix others, neither is it healthy for us to be in a relationship where we think we can.

Relationships should be mutually beneficial, supportive, nurturing and challenging in the very best way and to each other's highest purpose. This is true in both personal and professional relationships. Outside of these parameters it gets messy quickly.

Of course, deciding you will not engage, or stay, in toxic relationships does not mean you will never encounter one again.

"No one can make you feel inferior without your consent." Eleanor Roosevelt

TOXIC COMES IN MANY COLOURS

Early in my career as a financial advisor, I had a toxic client experience. It was my first year without a salary and I was relying on commissions to pay the bills. I only had a few clients, but one of them was a solid revenue generator that helped take the pressure off me financially.

He was a middle-aged lawyer who acted as Trustee for a wealthy individual. He opened an account with me to trade stocks with a very specific strategy and guidelines. It was a great learning experience for me; I followed the strategy and spent a considerable amount of time every day researching stocks and looking for opportunities to make money for my client.

He wanted to talk to me daily and meet weekly for lunch. Given the amount of trading we did, I thought this was reasonable and just part of the job. One day he asked if I'd like to go for a run with him after work. He said it would be a good opportunity to further discuss strategy while getting to know one another better, and get in shape at the same time. He was married with kids, so I didn't think anything of it. The other advisors in my office would spend hours golfing with their clients or engaging in other activities to forge stronger relationships that helped them build their businesses. I didn't see going for a run in any different light than that.

The difference was that I wasn't the same as the other advisors; I was a young woman working hard to break through some tough barriers. My client used this as an opportunity to take advantage of the situation. As we continued to meet often and went on a few runs together, I was starting to get the impression he was looking for more than just a business relationship. He hadn't tried or asked for anything more, but my spidey senses were on high alert.

Finally I just couldn't take it anymore. I didn't feel right earning commissions from a relationship based on something other than my ability as a financial advisor.

It was unethical and I needed to address it head on.

I had to psych myself up to confront the situation. What if I was wrong? How will he react? My heart was racing and I felt a knot in my stomach. I was worried that maybe I was reading the situation wrong. Over one of our regular lunches I decided to come right out and ask him why he was dealing with me. I said if it is because I'm good at my job, great, but if it is because he is attracted to me and was hoping for more, I would rather refer him to another advisor.

He assured me he was dealing with me because I was good at my job. At least, that's what he said. I apologized for bringing it up. My gut was still telling me otherwise, but it made me feel better as I made it clear that I was only interested in a professional relationship.

The next day I received a letter.

I was horrified to read it: six pages of slime confirming my spidey senses were functioning on full alert. At its tamest, he likened me to the football player who doesn't go out for beers with the team after the game or the doctor who doesn't make house calls. At its most revolting, he described the ways he thought of me sexually and how he couldn't fathom the idea of continuing to work with me without becoming intimate. I'll spare you the rest, but let's just say that I desperately needed a shower after reading it.

I took the letter to my manager.

I asked him to send a formal letter to this client informing him that he is no longer welcome at our firm and that we expect to receive a transfer out request immediately. I wanted to make sure that his account wasn't simply transferred to another advisor at our firm. No matter how much his commissions generated for an advisor or for the firm, I did not want to run into him in our office, ever.

My manager was very supportive and not only sent the letter, but covered the cost for me to seek a legal opinion as we were both concerned that he might continue to cause problems and make me feel unsafe. It felt good to know that I was doing something to try and stop him from taking advantage of other women.

I felt empowered, even though I didn't know how I was going to make up the lost revenue. It was the right decision without a doubt, but I could see why some people might feel financially trapped into continuing with a toxic relationship.

He continued to try and contact me on and off for a few years, but I not only ignored his attempts, I filed a police report in case he pursued further.

Having the courage to stand up for what is right will build confidence and lead you down a brighter path.

 *Trusting your gut is often the first step in recognizing a potential issue.*

My business grew considerably after that incident and I believe that was another turning point for me as I discovered I had what it takes to stand up for myself in what was considered a man's world. It reinforced my values and confirmed I couldn't be bought. Had I not left Tom and gone through that personal growth experience, I'm not sure this story would have had the same outcome.

Toxic relationships aren't always the obvious ones like I described previously. Often they can be subtle and those are the most difficult ones to acknowledge and eliminate.

Take for instance the long-time friend who always seems to be in a negative state of mind, complaining about something in her life. After a while, this becomes very draining and may start to bring you down as well. It's one thing to be there for a friend who is legitimately going through a rough patch; it's another to continue to spend time with someone who is always negative.

 *It's important to surround ourselves with positive and supportive people who believe in you.*

Being around the right people can bring out the very best in you, and you can bring out the best in others. It's a positive cycle that helps make every day better.

Letting go of people can be hard, especially if they have been in your life for a very long time. But it needs to be done to free up capacity for the right people at each stage in your life.

People come and go over the years, and that's okay. There's a saying that people come into your life for a reason, a season or a lifetime. I truly believe that. I believe we meet the right people at the right time as we need different people at different stages of our life to help us grow. People naturally go their separate ways when there is no longer a need for that relationship. This isn't a bad thing.

We can't continue to meet new people and build new relationships and expect to have enough time to keep everyone in our life. Think about all the people you have met in your lifetime thus far. What would your life look like if you were expected to stay in touch with all of them? It's not possible. The true friends will stay connected. They are the ones that you may not have spoken to for a long time, but can pick up the phone and pick up where you left off without any guilt or remorse.

When you feel constantly frustrated by someone with each encounter, it's usually caused by one of two things: that person is not a fit or you're just stressed. If you can rule out stress, the next step is to see if improved communication can eliminate the frustration. If not, it might be time to eliminate the relationship.

As an employer, this comes up when you have the wrong person in a certain role. It can be difficult to identify and resolve. In most cases it's better for both parties to deal with the issue as soon as possible so that both can move on.

Unfortunately, our desire to be liked (or a fear of being disliked) can get in the way of doing what's right. Get past it. Imagine your life without that person in it. Can you breathe deeper? Does it feel like a load has been lifted?

When it comes to family, disengaging can be even more challenging. You can't pick your family, but you can decide who to spend time with, how often, how long. We put pressure on ourselves to always put family first. While I fully agree with this when it comes to the people we love, I don't believe it must apply to all family members. If a family member is abusive, it's a toxic relationship and it needs to be eliminated from your life.

Abuse comes in many forms: physical, mental, emotional, and financial. If you find yourself trying too hard to make a relationship work, it might be time to ask yourself if it's worth it.

When deciding who should be in your life and who shouldn't, ask yourself what the relationship brings to the table. It should feel good, you should enjoy each other's company and there should be mutual benefit.

Take the risk of having fewer people to call or who call you —you will be surprised to discover you don't feel more alone, rather, your life feels richer and fuller with higher quality relationships than it did with all those high maintenance ones.

Look at the relationships in your life and run a cost/benefit analysis on all of them. Make your decision and stick with it. This might sound a little cold, but when you are surrounded by the right people it feels warm and fuzzy.

I never thought I would end any chapter with the words 'warm and fuzzy '.

It sure beats being miserable.

"I can't think of any better representation of beauty than someone who is unafraid to be herself." Emma Stone

CONFIDENCE

Simply put, confidence is a belief in yourself and your abilities. It comes more easily for some than it does for others, but it can come to all who seek it.

Confident people have a clear understanding and appreciation of their strengths and are comfortable with the reality that they don't know everything. They are willing to learn and don't need the spotlight to assure themselves of their worth. Confident people are people of conviction, self-possession, and courage. Confidence is a mindset. And a mindset is something you have full control over.

Why are some women more confident than others? Are you the type of person who takes the stage or hides behind the curtains? Which one do you want to be?

What does confidence look like to you? Do you speak quietly? Speak with your head down? Or do you stand tall, look people in the eye, and speak with conviction? Do you ask for what you want? Do you at least let it be known what you want?

I once read that the difference between confidence and arrogance is competence. I had to really think about that statement at first, but I couldn't agree more. We've all met people who come across as arrogant—the 'I-Know-It-All' or 'I'm-the-Best' type. Really, they are just trying to compensate for their insecurities or lack of competence. I think they lack self-awareness. I can't help but think that if they knew how others perceived them, they would change.

On the flip side, many women are concerned with how others perceive them and they worry about coming across as arrogant, so they downplay their strengths. This is sometimes perceived as lack of confidence, which can dramatically limit opportunities.

 *People want to work with confident people.*

If I'm hiring someone new, I want that person to exude confidence and deliver performance. In the financial services industry it is crucial to be confident and competent. No matter how competent the person might be, if they can't come across as confident, they will fail. Would you invest your money with a professional who had a mousy voice and who sounded apologetic for their recommendations?

Of course, there is a double standard when it comes to assertiveness. Men who are assertive or even aggressive are respected and rewarded. Women who are assertive are seen as aggressive and called a 'bitch'—and often with a capital B. I think this holds many women back from saying what they really mean. You don't have to be a Bitch. You can be aggressive yet kind. We can change this perception by having the confidence to state our mind and by supporting one another in the process. If this becomes the norm, the double standard will disappear.

Independence builds confidence. It's not a good place to be dependent on others in ways that limit you. The psychology of co-dependence, dependence, inter-dependence and independence are beyond the scope and point of this chapter, but suffice it to say that healthy relationships thrive on valuing independence and nurture confidence. Toxic ones don't.

I used to work with a young man who said he would only date women he thought were slightly less attractive than he perceived himself to be. He scored himself an eight out of ten as a man, so he preferred to date women that he thought society would rate as a seven out of ten. This sounded ridiculous to me because we often see older unattractive men with young bombshells in an attempt to puff their egos (don't get me started on that topic!)

I asked why he took that approach. He said it made him feel more confident and less worried about being dumped for someone more attractive. Wow. His insecurities and lack of confidence were negatively impacting his options for finding the right mate. The good news is that over time, with experience and maturity, he grew into a confident and successful man.

 *Building confidence can be easy. The payoff is immediate.*

Set small goals and achieve them. If your goal is to exercise three days this week, do it. Don't let yourself down. Do what you said you were going to do. Make sure you have blocked the time in your schedule to accommodate this goal and no matter how tired you feel, make yourself exercise those three times. At the end of the week, you'll feel better about yourself and your ability to follow-through on a goal. Whether it's a promise not to hit the snooze button for a whole week, or to cut out your Starbucks addiction for a month, set little goals and stick to them and your confidence will begin to grow.

Take things to the next level and look for new things to try or chances to take. Maybe it's applying for a new job, going back to school or entering an adventure race. Ask yourself, 'what's the worst that can happen' and 'what's the best that can happen?' And finally, 'If the worst case happens, would it really be a big deal?'

I recently met a woman on a flight to Calgary. She is married with a couple of kids, yet this was the first time in her life she had travelled on her own. She was nervous about getting to the airport, changing planes in Calgary, and taking a taxi from the airport to her final destination. My first reaction was, 'Are you for real? It's no big deal!', but I put myself in her shoes.

She was a small town girl, nervous about being on her own in a bigger city—worried about all the things that could go wrong rather than what might go right. By talking it through, I helped her think through some solutions. If she missed her connecting flight, she'd be delayed a few hours, but would still get to where she was going. I couldn't help but think how good this experience would be for her to build confidence and to know that she can be independent.

 *Self-confidence can be built or eroded.*

Lack of confidence usually coincides with a fear of failure and a lack of trust in oneself. I felt my own confidence erode during the time I was with Tom. I started questioning myself and was afraid to make the right choices. When I finally broke free and overcame my fear of leaving and moving to a new city, my confidence grew.

Each time we compromise our truth, our instinct, what we know to be right and wrong, our confidence in ourselves and our abilities to make good decisions tanks.

Being afraid can prevent you from trying, but you won't grow as a person without trying new things. Think of a situation you have been in where you felt insecure. Perhaps it was at a social function where you felt out of place and had no one to talk to. What was holding you back from meeting new people and introducing yourself? I would guess it was a fear of being rejected (or failing to be liked).

But wait! Aren't you already feeling rejected by sitting in the sidelines like a wallflower?

Take a chance and introduce yourself to a group of people. Try to find common interests and you'll be pleasantly surprised by how enjoyable the experience can be. Once you realize that your fear of being rejected wasn't rational, you'll start to build confidence and the whole process will get easier and easier. Next thing you know, maybe you'll be the life of the party!

When I first started as a financial advisor, I experienced that 'fear of failure' head on. To earn new business I needed to ask for it, but what if I was turned down? What if people think I'm too pushy or not smart enough? What if I don't know the answer to their questions? These were some of the thoughts that went through my mind, but I didn't let them prevent me from trying. I realized that by not asking for business, I wouldn't get anywhere.

Getting 'no' for an answer is the default to not taking action, so what did I have to lose?

In fact, my fear of failure pushed me into doing what it took to succeed. I knew I could deliver and had confidence in my ability, but was unsure of whether other people would see me that way or not.

I thought long and hard about how I could reach out to people that I wanted to connect with.

I formulated a strategy and key messaging to make the process a little easier. I prepared myself to handle rejection. I learned not to take it personally and reminded myself that not everyone is going to like me and I'm not going to like everyone. We're only human after all.

It wasn't easy at first. I like to please people and felt hurt when someone didn't want to work with me. Over time I realized that was silly. I won't be a fit for everyone. I need to focus my attention on those people who value my services.

I shifted my thinking to truly focus on the client and what they needed. From there I could develop a strategy to help clients achieve their goals, but if I didn't think I could add any value, I would say so and refer them to someone else. This further built trust in the client / advisor relationship and built confidence in my ability to deliver great service and results.

As I took action, I overcame my fears. As I did, I became who I wanted to be.

The more clients I met with, the more referrals I received for new clients and my confidence grew. Getting a few 'no's' along the way helped me learn and grow as an advisor. I had to put my personal feelings aside and look at the situation objectively. I asked myself what I could have done better. Did I take the time to truly get to know what was important to the client or did I jump into a sales pitch? Did I portray myself as confident and experienced or young and naïve?

Over time I learned that a 'no' almost always stems from a lack of perceived value. Clients need to see the value an advisor offers to them before they will agree to move ahead.

The same principle applies in other situations. Whether you're trying to get a promotion at work or get your kids to clean up their room, having the ability to get others to see the value and/or benefit to them is the key to getting the result you're looking for.

 *When it comes to building confidence "Fake it until you make it" is a pretty good strategy.*

Studies show that forcing yourself to smile can actually make you happier[6], and I believe the same thing holds true for confidence. If you adjust your posture to portray confidence, you will likely feel more confident as a result.

Here's a tip: prior to facing a situation that makes you nervous, find a private place where you can stand tall and raise your arms above your head as you tell yourself out loud 'I've got this.' Make yourself as big as possible and speak loudly. You'll feel weird at first, but it'll give you the boost you need. You might even laugh at yourself, but that's good too!

I had some swagger early in my career as I enjoyed what I was doing and it showed. A big part of that came from my belief in who I am and my ability to deliver. I hadn't done it a million times yet for a lot of different people, but I knew I could do it. It came from being aware of and okay with what I don't know. I had the drive to find answers. I made sure that was the Sybil every client (existing or prospective) saw. They had to see the strong, confident financial advisor who had the answers to their questions or knew where to find them.

I understood the weight of the responsibility in managing people's life savings. I took it seriously and beat them to the punch on any doubts they had. I would say

---

6 https://web.psych.ualberta.ca

at our first meeting, 'I may appear young, but I was born to do this. I am good at math, a natural problem solver, have energy and will work very hard to help you succeed and achieve your financial goals.'

Tackling the issue head-on seemed to make it go away. We could focus on the issue at hand, which was building their portfolio, not how old I was.

 *Confident people are authentic and don't claim to know all the answers. They're not afraid to be themselves.*

When you're in conversation with someone who's confident, they tend to listen more and take an interest in others. They don't need to prove themselves because they already feel good about who they are. It allows for a natural curiosity about others.

Arrogant people tend to act better than they are and pretend to know more than they do. It's all about them. An arrogant person will talk almost nonstop and not really care to listen to what the other person is saying, because they're trying to get other people to like them or be impressed by them. They're looking to be served rather than to be of service.

People are attracted to confidence and repelled by arrogance. Arrogance almost always reveals an insecure, incompetent person. You may be trying to fake it 'til you make it, but when you cross over into arrogance, you're not pulling it off, as it doesn't align with the right values.

You need to be curious to be confident, and you need to have an awareness and recognition that you're never done learning. Confident people don't have all the answers; they just know where to find them or are humble enough to admit when they are out of their area of expertise. There's no way any one person can know everything there is to know about everything. Confident people can admit that.

In other words, don't B.S. – people pick up on it and the consequences are bad if you are wrong.

If you don't know what you're talking about, just say so. It's better to say, 'I want to give this a little more thought because it's too important an issue for me to speak off the top of my head,' or, 'I have a few different solutions that I'm thinking of, I'm going to get back to you on that', than it is to try and make something up on the spot. Confidence comes from knowing it's okay to not always have the answers at your fingertips.

The most successful people thrive on continuous learning and are always looking to improve. They hire personal and/or business coaches to help make them even better. It astonishes me the number of underachievers I meet who refuse to take a course, attend a conference or hire a coach because they feel they already know it all.

People who don't have a degree tend to feel less confident than those who do, especially in the business world.

I was speaking to a woman the other day who wanted to apply for a leadership position at a firm. She was discouraged by the job description because it stated a preference for candidates with an undergraduate degree. She had many of the skills for the job, she just didn't have a degree. She had fifteen years relative experience and decided to apply for the position anyway.

Kudos to her because given her experience, having a degree didn't really matter. Even after I told her this, it was nagging at her and she asked if she should get a degree anyway.

I told her that If the degree would help her perform better then sure; if it's simply to impress other people, then no.

If the degree would make her feel good about herself and she had the time to get it done without taking away from other priorities, then okay.

Setting goals and achieving them are what employers look for. Getting results is the end goal.

A degree shows an ability to learn, demonstrates drive, dedication and self-discipline—all great qualities. It's not the degree itself; it's what it took to get there that's important.

I've worked with a number of women over the years who don't have degrees and are insecure about it. Okay, if you don't have a degree, why didn't you get it? And how important is it really at this point in time? Is it the content you want to learn or are you concerned with what other people think of you? Is having a degree in art literature relevant to business?

Focus on the other things you have accomplished, courses you've completed and lessons learned. You may find it adds up to something more relevant than that piece of paper. You may find you possess the same benefits of a degree but that you just went a different route. That being said, if you have the time and money—if obtaining a degree will build your confidence or provide you with career-advancing opportunities—go for it.

I love challenging myself to try new things and the feeling I get when I succeed at something I've put my mind to. It feels good to have a checklist and cross things off as they get done. It builds confidence. I look at the people I admire and ask myself, what can I do to be someone people look up to? Having role models makes me a better role model for others.

Find a role model, someone who inspires you, and use that person to coax you out of your comfort zone and to try something new. Find a mutually beneficial connection so you can seek their advice and return the favour by showcasing their successes or helping them with a project or event.

One of my role models is a local, successful entrepreneur. I invited her to speak at an International Women's Day event we were hosting. She was pleased to be asked and was happy to accept as she loved helping people be the best that they can be.

This initial introduction turned into a relationship. We connect for lunch a couple of times per year and pick each other's brain on topics of importance. We always leave our meetings feeling inspired to take action on a new goal (more on goals later in this book).

Whether you are driven to be the best mom you can be or to climb the corporate ladder, set goals and push yourself to learn and improve. Each time you try something new or mark something off your to-do list, you build confidence.

Keeping promises to yourself and others is equally important. Do what you say you are going to do.

When you let yourself down, it feels terrible. Be reasonable with your promises, start small, and stick to them. If you make a mistake along the way, face it, fix it and recalibrate. If your goal is to lose ten pounds, break it into smaller pieces and let yourself enjoy several milestones along the way. Perhaps it's losing one pound per week for ten weeks. That is a very achievable goal and every week you accomplish it, you'll feel great.

The most important tip for building confidence is to step out of your comfort zone. Just a little bit is enough to get started.

Never tell yourself that a goal is too small to matter. If you can push yourself to do things that you are nervous about, you'll feel fantastic about yourself when you achieve that goal.

Start small and work your way up. The more you do, the more confidence you'll build.

On that note, it also seems appropriate to add a sidebar on dressing for success. There are plenty of books on the topic, so I'll keep it brief. The simple truth is that I feel more confident when I'm dressed for the occasion. Why? Because first impressions matter. Of course people shouldn't "judge a book by its cover", but the reality is: people judge. Even if you're in an entry level position, you may think no one cares and you can dress for yourself. But what you wear makes a statement that is judged instantly. While no one will comment or notice when you're dressed appropriately (and there are a wide range of options to do so), the moment you dress inappropriately —too provocatively, too casual, too glittery — you're making a statement that people will notice. And not in a good way.

Yes, you can still dress for yourself. But make sure it says what you want people to think about you. It seems that the rules of dressing appropriately for men are a lot clearer than the rules for women. Men need a clean shirt, pants that fit, socks (in most industries) and shoes. For women it's a wide open minefield. Here are my simple rules:

1) Style has no price tag (you don't need to spend a fortune)

2) Size and age are not style factors (dress appropriately)

3) Good is good and less is more (less meaning simple, not less coverage)

The key is to embrace your personality, know what you value and why, use it as your anchor and let it guide you. If you're not sure, ask a friend. There are plenty of shops with style consultants who can help. There's no need to go this one alone.

Self-confidence is the best outfit. Rock it and own it.

MONEY

Why do you do what you do?

This is a tough question. It requires digging deep within yourself to find total, unfiltered honesty. Most will answer with what they think is a socially acceptable answer. People don't like to be judged and have an innate desire to be liked. This isn't a bad thing, but be careful you don't hold yourself back in fear of what others might think. If you are driven by money, for example, others might judge you as greedy or shallow. I challenge you to think deeper to get to your true values. Is it the money you like or the power that comes with it?

Different people have different values. I'm going to say that title and money drive men, and women are driven more by compassion and caretaking —maybe a sense of accomplishment if they've helped someone else. The caretaking approach seems to come more naturally to women—you know what I mean—asking if you need anything, and always thinking of other peoples' needs before their own.

I am not driven by money. I like money. There is a difference. I enjoy the money I make: I get to go on nice holidays, live in a nice house and get to support charitable causes I believe in. I help other people make the most out of their life and that's rewarding, but it's not the dollars that drive me. It's the challenge and the goal of it.

I'm happy in the moment of doing what I'm doing and the dollars just come. Look at athletes. Do you think they are driven by the dollars they make? Or are they driven by being recognized as being the best and the status that comes along with that? OK, maybe we'll get mixed answers on that one, but you know what I'm getting at.

Happiness is living your life your way, not measured by dollars, title or fame. If you spend less than you earn, you'll always have enough money.

When you are driven by dollars only, you might make poor decisions along the way that can take you away from your true passion and set your life gets off balance. Remember money is only one piece of life. If you spend all your effort and energy on that piece, what's going to happen to the rest?

Different people need different amounts of money.

I have multi-millionaire clients. Some of them are happy, but not all of them. The ones who are happy are the ones who do what they love—the money has just come as a side effect. But I know a few multi-millionaires who are never satisfied. They are driven so much by money that they do things they don't like. They aren't enjoying the journey, they spend more than they need and, to add insult to injury, are not even happy spending it.

On the other end of the spectrum, I have clients who are happy on almost nothing. I advised a couple who lived in a small community in a little house and their idea of fun includes fishing and driving across Canada in their camper truck. They spend a great deal of time with their grandkids and engage in low cost hobbies to fill their days. Their needs are simple and what makes them happy doesn't cost a lot of money. If they won the lottery, they would give most of it away to their kids and charity. They are living the life they want. Life couldn't be better.

Even though my parents offered to assist financially, I put myself through school. They had managed to save a few thousand dollars to help pay for my tuition and books.

They offered to let me continue to live at home for free, but I wanted to live on my own. I didn't feel right taking money from my parents when I knew I could do it myself. I was fortunate enough to have a good part-time job as a pharmacy technician and qualified for student loans to cover my tuition and books.

Mom would bring over bags of groceries from time to time, for which I was extremely grateful!

I was scraping by, but I was on my own and loving it.

I suggested my parents should use the money they had saved for my education and go on a vacation instead. They'd never really been anywhere, so they took me up on it and went to Bali. It made me feel really good to see them enjoying life.

I continued to work hard after graduation and it didn't take me long to pay off my student loan. I took pride in doing it myself and the result was an increase in self-confidence. The feeling of accomplishment after achieving a goal encouraged me to set even more goals. Goals not just for me, but for my family.

I was driven by the sense of accomplishment and the good feeling of seeing someone else enjoy life. To be the one who suggested an opportunity to someone else and to see that person realize it is amazing. I couldn't help but see opportunities when it came to finances. It's just the way my brain is wired. To be able to share that skillset with my family was great.

Being the numbers nerd that I am, I started looking into real estate opportunities when I was eighteen years old. At that time, my parents owned a modest family home, with the mortgage almost paid off. Since I was living on my own and my sister was in high school, they were starting to think that they had more house than they needed. We talked about converting the basement to a suite to generate rental income.

I took it one step further and started looking into rental properties in other parts of the city. I found a few that caught my eye as the rental income was great and they were located in desirable areas. I started showing the listings to my parents and helped them run the numbers. The value of these properties was considerably higher than their current home, but I explained that the rental income would pay for the difference and down the road they would have a larger asset to sell and retire on. Mom was out of her comfort zone. Dad was more comfortable as he could see what it would mean for their future. After much discussion and looking at several properties, they decided to take the plunge. It worked out as planned.

At twenty-one, this inspired me to look into buying a house instead of renting. I was living with my boyfriend, Chad (now my husband), and we were saving to go on a trip around the world. With a healthy sum in our bank account, we decided to use that as a downpayment on a home instead. We figured we could travel later, but getting into the real estate market at that time would set us up better for the future. Money was tight. I was working on my degree and only working part time, but the house we bought had a rental suite to help cover our mortgage payments. We needed my parents to co-sign for the mortgage, but we were officially homeowners. We still managed to travel, albeit on smaller trips and cheaper hotels.

Several years later, real estate valuations had increased substantially but rental income hadn't. My parents were getting tired of being landlords. I re-ran the numbers. The net income as a percentage of market value wasn't as attractive as it had once been. It now made sense to sell, take the profit and downsize into a house more suitable for their retirement years. The sale made enough money to create a retirement income stream.

And so it began for me. I didn't know it yet, but I was going to do very well as a financial advisor helping people make the most out of what they have.

I always thought that because I was good at math and numbers, I would be an accountant. After a couple of accounting courses I realized it wasn't for me. There were aspects I enjoyed, like tax saving strategies, but overall I found it a bit dry. I didn't want to spend my days behind the scenes. I liked the big picture. I liked to set big goals and work backwards to do the things needed to achieve those goals. I'm a planner by nature, as I believe many women are, which is why the financial services industry is often a great fit for women. That being said, according to Cerulli Associates, 86% of financial advisors are male[7]. It's time for that to change.

Money is a side effect of being driven to be the best you can be with what you are good at. I challenge people to discover this for themselves.

 *Be driven to be the best you can be, whatever that is, and the right amount of money will come.*

7 http://www.fa-mag.com/news/wanted--women-financial-advisors-25321.html

POSSIBILITIES

As a girl I knew I wanted to run my own business, work with people and numbers, but didn't know exactly what that meant or where to start. I started walking down the path by signing up for a few general courses at the local college, but then it hit me, I should get a business degree. I had a surge of energy and focus that was previously missing. I signed up for all the first-year transfer courses and achieved the A- average required for acceptance into the business school at the University of Victoria. From there, everything became clear. I had set my sights on something. I had a goal to achieve. I didn't know what specific career path I wanted, but I was confident that a business degree would lead me in the right direction.

What really steered me in the right direction was the mandatory co-op work experience through the Peter B. Gustavson School of Business at the University of Victoria.

I had left getting a co-op placement until the last minute and was scrambling to find something fast. The process was to look at the job postings and apply through the Co-op office. The Co-op director would weed through the resumes and only forward the most suitable candidates to each employer, based on the best match of skillsets. As I was looking at the postings on a bulletin board, the director suggested I bypass the normal process and go down to one of the employers in person. What a great idea! I went home, put on my best suit (okay, my only suit at the time) and walked into a brokerage firm called Midland Walwyn.

I had never worked in an office and knew nothing about the company, so I grabbed a few brochures from their lobby and went outside to prepare myself with some background knowledge. (This was before the days of Google.) I marched back into the office and asked the receptionist if I could speak to the hiring manager, and explained I was from the Faculty of Business. I didn't clarify whether I was a student or staff, but wasn't asked and it did the trick.

The hiring manager came to greet me and invited me into her office. I introduced myself as a student who is very interested in the position available and asked her what the job entailed and the type of candidate she was looking for. I convinced her that my work experience as a pharmacy technician made me the perfect candidate to cover her maternity leave as the branch administrator. This sounds ridiculous, but it makes sense if you look at the transferrable skills and a willing-to-learn attitude.

As a pharmacy technician I was responsible for customer service, professional interactions with doctors and pharmacists, privacy issues, security in regards to handling narcotics, accurate filing and record keeping, computer skills and problem solving. Those were all skills required in the role she was hiring for. By meeting me in person, she formed a good first impression, much better than she would have had by reading my resume alone. She called me the following morning to offer me the job. I was thrilled! My first task was to type and send a 'Thanks for applying, but the position has been filled' letter to my peers.

Once on the job, I was introduced to a career path I didn't know existed. My parents didn't have much investment experience, and no one had ever introduced me to the concept of investing. I knew about saving, which meant putting money in the bank for future use, but that is very different from investing. Buying and selling stocks was a foreign concept, but I was instantly fascinated and wanted to learn everything I could about making money and helping others do the same. I watched advisors build investment portfolios to help clients achieve their goals and I knew this would be a good fit for me. I got to fix things that people didn't know were broken and help investors seize opportunities. I started working on the courses I would need to pursue a career as a financial advisor.

The Co-op was 4 months, and being the go-getter that I am, I also took two business classes while working full time. It's amazing what we are capable of accomplishing when we are driven. I knew what I wanted to do and what was needed to get there. I worked hard to get it done as quickly as possible. My first Co-op turned into a second term. I took three more business courses and completed the Canadian Securities Course at the same time. I wanted to complete my degree so that I could focus on my career.

When I look back, I sometimes wonder how I fit it all in, but the same thing applies in my life today. I am happiest when working toward a goal or multiple goals. I had a fire in my belly to complete my degree and that desire fueled me with the energy needed to get it done quickly.

A fun exercise is to ask yourself: 'what would I do if I won $20 million dollars in the lottery'? All of a sudden, the financial pressures are gone and anything is possible. This takes you out of your current reality and limited mindset into a new world of possibilities. This is when you can get creative and truly find the things that are important to you.

Many people say things like: travel, buy a house (or pay off a mortgage), buy a new car, help friends and family, invest the money and live off the interest and/or give to a specific charity. I've heard people say they'd hire a personal chef and trainer to get healthy.

The good news is that you do not need to win the lottery to achieve the goals you've set from this exercise. Your house may be smaller, your trips less extravagant, but you can still accomplish them. Thinking about the possibilities is often enough to kick-start the desire for something, which leads to the drive to obtain it, which leads to accomplishing what you initially desired.

After my two work terms, I had full-time job offers as an assistant to numerous advisors. I wanted to finish my degree first because I knew it would be harder to complete later if I put it off. I took a part time job as an assistant to the top-producing advisor in the branch. I was able to complete my degree and learn from the best at the same time. It turns out that he wasn't the best in the way he ran his business, and I actually learned a lot about what not to do from him, but that was also of great value.

By the time I finished my degree, I had built up my industry experience, completed the Canadian Securities Course, earned my Professional Financial Planning designation and my Canadian Investment Management designation. I was now ready to focus on my career. The exciting part for me was that a career as a financial advisor encompasses all the things that I wanted in one career path:

- own my own business
- problem solve
- work with people
- work with numbers
- help others
- have unlimited earning potential

What a perfect fit. As a financial advisor, I help people visualize their future and put a plan in place to achieve their goals. Whether it's helping someone retire, buy a vacation home, travel around the world or send their kids to university, it's my job to help make it come true. It's very rewarding and fuels my drive to not only build and manage my own wealth, but to help people make the most out of what they have and achieve their goals. If I make other people happy, I am happy.

The hardest part of the financial industry, and this holds true with most businesses, is actually finding the clients. You've got to convince people that you know what you're doing, and that you're the best solution for them. After all, you're asking them to trust you with their life savings. If you add to that being a young female in a male-dominated industry, and being told by almost everyone else you're going to fail—you have some serious obstacles to overcome.

Even my mother doubted me, asking 'Why would you give up a secure job with benefits and a salary to be an advisor on your own where you're commission-based and there is no steady income?'

It was clear to me that I was born to be an advisor. I had all the right attributes: a natural problem solver, good with numbers, strong business sense and a passion for helping people. Mom is risk averse. She doesn't gamble or take chances as she prefers to have a safe and stable income. I knew myself well enough to understand that taking the safe, lower paying job would bore me.

In my opinion, since we spend the majority of our waking hours working, it better be something we love to do.

Even though others around me were concerned about me failing as an advisor, I knew deep within that I had what it took and I was going to do everything I could to succeed. I wasn't afraid of hard work or asking for help. I wanted to prove the naysayers wrong, to show them that yes, I can do what I put my mind to and hopefully that would inspire them to try something new as well.

I was fully aware that the stats were against me, but I was so confident in my ability to deliver and had an overwhelmingly strong desire to succeed, that the obstacles shrunk into the background. I kept focusing on the end goal and that pushed me forward.

IN A MAN'S WORLD

Most advisors in the financial industry when I started were men. That hasn't changed.

There are a number of reasons why women haven't made inroads:

- lack of role modeling for young women that this is a great career path
- lack of awareness that this is a viable career option for women
- lack of support by many firms to meet the specific needs of women in this industry (flexible hours, remote work access, mentorship and training)

Although employers are not allowed to ask young women if they plan to have a family, the reality is that it crosses their minds and negatively impacts hiring women. It's about time this changed.

Women of child-bearing age are considered a liability in the workplace and get passed over for promotions because they might one day have a baby. Women who have worked hard and proven their worth to companies often take maternity leave only to return to find their position has been eliminated (often a code for reassigned to someone else under a different title).

The 'Old Boys Club' saw me as an assistant not as an advisor, and as a result did not treat me equally. I was often asked to fetch the coffee or expected to tidy up the kitchen. In branch meetings, I was the one they asked to take notes since I was the only female advisor.

I'm happy to grab a coffee, tidy the kitchen or take notes as long as it's on an equitable basis whereby the men do their share. That wasn't the case, so I had to handle the situation tactfully. I remember taking notes at one meeting, but kicked off the next meeting by asking one of the men to take notes. This came as a bit of a surprise to the group, but it worked.

This was a challenge in the workplace, as well as in bringing in new clients. I knew I had to go above and beyond to win trust and confidence in order to break these unconscious biases. Once given the opportunity to speak and demonstrate I knew my stuff, I'm smart and I could help them make money, they listened and started treating me equally.

I did a financial projection for every client, something that very few advisors at that time did. This process helped clients clearly see what was possible and what they needed to do to achieve their goals. Without the financial projections, many clients would never have known what to do differently and would therefore not achieve some of the great things they wanted to. The plan fueled their desire which led to drive and action to get results. It gave them confidence in me.

I found that I had to know more than my male counterparts to be heard and given the opportunity to be treated equally. I took extra courses and earned more designations than the average advisor.

But even just getting that door open in the first place was a bit of a challenge. Once I made my mind up to become a financial advisor, I was turned down by the firm I worked for. I was told by an older male colleague that I shouldn't even bother becoming an advisor because I would fail. The failure rate for new advisors was high, only twenty percent were still in the business five years after starting. He said to me 'Sybil, Sybil Sybil...what do you want to be an advisor for? This is a really tough business and the failure rate is high. On top of that, you have three things going against you that the rest of us don't: you're young, you're female, and you're pretty. People just won't take you seriously.'

I was initially crushed, but that only lasted for about two seconds before it turned into anger. I used that anger to fuel my desire to succeed.

> *"I never dreamed about success. I worked for it."* Estee Lauder

DRIVE

The advisor I was assisting at the time decided to move firms and needed me to help set up the new office. If I agreed to move with them, I would be offered the position of branch administrator. Since I had already decided I really wanted to be a financial advisor, I turned them down. They were in a difficult position as they needed my administrative knowledge and skillset to help ensure a successful transition to the new firm. Out of desperation, they agreed to hire me as an advisor at the new firm if I would help them transition first. Perfect! Here was my opportunity to move forward in my career.

The transition took longer than expected, but after a year, I finally got what I wanted and was granted the role of financial advisor. The firm had never hired a 'rookie' before and weren't sure how to structure the compensation. Financial advisors don't make a salary; they earn a percentage of the revenue they generate for the firm. The firm offered to pay me a small base salary, but I declined. I didn't want to be treated differently. I wanted to be treated with the same respect the other advisors received. I therefore decided to be paid the same way everyone else was. This was a bit scary as I had no idea how I was going to generate income at the beginning, but I was empowered because I would have only myself to blame if things didn't work out.

Without the safety net of a salary, I was even more driven to succeed.

While I was getting the new office established, I had time to formulate a business plan for growing my own business. I paid close attention to what successful advisors did well and I planned and developed a service system that I would use for my clients.

Since I was working for a bank-owned investment comany, I would have the opportunity to work with the local bank branches to get referrals, but the other advisors in our office weren't likely to share with me. I asked my manager if I could work with the bank branch in Campbell River (a four hour drive away), and he said I could fill my boots.

I had a brother-in-law living in that small town, so my plan was to drive up Monday morning and home Tuesday night. His family welcomed me with a place to sleep each week. On my first trip there, I introduced myself to the bank manager and asked if he had an office I could use to start growing my business. He said I could use one of the spare offices, but that they didn't have any business for me. I said not to worry, I would be drumming up my own business and I just needed a place to meet clients.

My next stop was at the local library to research the town's demographics and get a feel for where the opportunities might be. After showing up in the office two days every week, it wasn't long before the bankers started referring some business to me as I could offer their clients services they didn't have access to. I held seminars, did mail drops and attended some networking events to drum up more business. I ended up hiring a full time assistant in Victoria to answer my phone, manage my schedule, and process paperwork. Since I was just starting out, I had no idea how I was going to pay her, but I was prepared to go into debt the first year to make things work. Short-term pain, long-term gain. As it turned out, I never had a month where I couldn't pay her. My business just took off.

I was working hard, and it was paying off. I felt great.

One day, the colleague that had told me I would fail popped into my office and said 'Sybil, Sybil, Sybil, what are you doing? I must say I am impressed with your success and even a bit jealous. How are you signing up so many clients? Well, you do have three things going for you that we don't: you're young, female and pretty. That must be working for you.'

I was giggling inside, but didn't feel the need to remind him those were the same three things he said would cause me to fail.

Don't let anyone else tell you what you are capable of... or not capable of. Follow your own path and shoot for your own goals.

New issues arose. My local manager tried to stop me from doing business in Nanaimo. Nanaimo was a town on my way to and from Campbell River, and it made sense for me to pop into the local bank branch to see if I could be of service. I was building a clientele there because it was an under-serviced market at the time, but my manager said I had to stop going there. This made no sense to me as he was paid an override on the business I did. Why would he want me to stop? He said the other advisors were jealous of my success.

I explained that I have clients there, and still needed to go to Nanaimo to see them. He agreed to allow me to continue seeing existing clients, but he didn't want me bringing in new clients. He was being completely unreasonable. At the time, I was the only advisor going to Nanaimo, so I suggested we open up all the bank branches on the island to allow advisors equal opportunity. He agreed and it allowed me to continue to bring in new business.

It was an arbitrary obstacle thrown in my way. And I had found a way around it. It boosted my confidence.

Incidentally, only one other advisor took advantage of the Nanaimo opportunity, but didn't experience the same success. Each of the other advisors had bank branches in Victoria they could visit but they weren't seeing much in the way of new client referrals. I think it was their approach. They tended to exude a sense of entitlement with the bank staff; it didn't go over well.

I took a 'team player' approach and referred a considerable amount of business back to the bankers. It's amazing how much better things can be when you create win-win scenarios.

At the beginning, when you're trying to build a business, it's common to take on anyone and everyone as a client. I couldn't afford to be choosy. I took on anyone with some money to invest and enjoyed helping them meet their needs, but that was spreading me a little bit too thin. I had to adjust over time. Once I had a solid base established, I was able to be more selective in choosing the clients I would work with.

I hate putting a price tag on clients that I deal with, because I love working with people. That being said, I can't work with everyone; there just aren't enough hours in the day. This is where I see many women struggle. We want to help everyone. Most women like to please and want to help people succeed. We have a hard time putting our businesses and ourselves first, which often leads to burnout, and then we're no good to anyone.

Finding the right balance and ensuring our priorities are in the right order ought to always be our guiding principle, but that is hard for so many of us to do.

We can help others while still putting our personal health first and pursuing a successful business or career.

Making ends meet kept me up at night in the beginning.

Since I had to negotiate my way into the role in the first place, I didn't want special treatment. I was driven to prove myself, yet there I was: twenty-five years old with no income, wondering how to make ends meet, but knowing I had to try.

Many people are so afraid of failure and so scared to try something new, that they wouldn't take the risk. I look at it differently. Most new businesses require a capital investment, but the financial services industry doesn't. Since I didn't need to take a loan, I was prepared to go into debt my first year instead. My husband was working and we had a line of credit, so if we had to go into debt twenty thousand dollars just to make ends meet that first year, we would. If we had to live on spaghetti and meatballs for a year, we were going to live on spaghetti and meatballs for a year. I thought it was a small price to pay for an incredible business opportunity. Chad earned enough to pay the mortgage and the basics with no frills, so I had a safety net.

I started thinking of this as an investment in our future rather than a risky endeavor.

Many of my friends at that time were buying new vehicles on credit, incurring twenty to thirty thousand dollars debt instantly, with only a depreciating asset to show for it. I continued to share a used vehicle with Chad that was paid for. I saw what we were doing with our line of credit as a much wiser investment that turned out to be a winner.

I was nervous, but I had a goal, I had a plan, and was focused on the desired result. Once I knew what I needed to do to achieve the goal, I executed on it. I had faith in my ability and a belief in myself that I could do it. I asked myself what's the worst that can happen and managed the risk accordingly. I would rather try and fail than not try and always wonder 'what if'.

I didn't let the fear paralyze me. I didn't let it get in the way of doing what I wanted to do. When someone jumps out of an airplane to skydive, they're scared, but often they do it again as it makes them feel good. Chad and I agreed to give it a year. Worst case scenario was that in twelve months we'd have some debt and I'd be looking for a new job. Chad wholeheartedly believed in me. Having a support network added a level of security and encouragement. And so I did it. January 1, 1999, was day one of me being an advisor on commission.

Drive is the desire to achieve a goal. Without desire, there is no drive. What is it that drives you? If you're not sure or it's been a while since you've asked yourself this question, it's time to uncover or re-discover the answer.

 *Aim high, get over your fears, believe in yourself. More importantly, just get off your ass and do it.*

"If you want something said, ask a man. If you want something done, ask a woman." Margaret Thatcher

THAT VENUS MARS THING

Men and women really are different. While I write this book, I'm trying to figure out whether the difference is learned behaviour or something we're born with.

Since I've always had an 'I can do anything' mindset, I thought everyone did. Turns out they don't.

I've interviewed a number of successful women. I honestly believed that the strong successful women would have more 'male traits' than 'female traits' when it came to career ambitions, but I was surprised by my findings.

It's not that women aren't also somewhat motivated by money and title, but it's not at the top of the list like it is for men that I've interviewed. The most successful women admitted they were driven more by impact in other people's lives than their own title and pay grade. When following their passions and doing what's right for others, the income and title followed. Looking back, that absolutely applies to me as well.

 *Unconscious biases can cause leaders to miss out on solid talent right in front of them.*

Of course men and women are different, and we should embrace those difference and work together for mutual benefit.

Those differences, however, have led to some unconscious biases that have long informed our societal beliefs. We need to address those unconscious biases and ask whether they still apply today, or if they have lost their relevancy and need to be changed?

Recently I took a helicopter flight from Vancouver to Victoria and was pleasantly surprised to see two female pilots. I was impressed and asked about the stats for women in their profession. They informed me that only about 3.5% of commercial pilots in Canada are female.

That evening I told my mother-in-law about it and her first response was, 'Were you scared?' I laughed. I thought she was kidding. She wasn't. She added (as though imparting a universal truth) that there are some things men are just better at.

I was horrified, but realized she was speaking purely from social conditioning. As evidenced by my textbook landing in Victoria, I was no less safe with two women in the cockpit than I would have been with two men, but my mother-in-law represents a significant part of the population who still subscribes, whether unconsciously or not, to these archetypes. This type of conditioning is exactly what needs to change.

When our son was born, my husband took parental leave. I did not. We both faced a range of negative judgments from poorly disguised 'jokes' to outright criticism.

- My husband was the first firefighter in the City of Victoria to take parental leave—a prime reason to tease. He was asked if his nipples were sore. All in good fun, of course.
- Many women couldn't believe I didn't take time off. They wondered about the importance of breastfeeding and how I would incorporate

that into my schedule.

One woman told me she thought it was wrong that I didn't take a maternity leave as a 'baby needs his mother'. Wow. I agree that babies need love and nurturing, but it shouldn't fall completely on the mother. Women can pump breastmilk so the fathers can feed the babies and build a bond. Formula is another option, one that we adopted within the first few weeks as it was a convenient option that allowed more freedom and flexibility.

 *There is more than one right way to raise children and each family will make the choices that work best for them.*

In 2017, as I write this book, parental leave is not only encouraged, but expected of men in Norway[8]. A ten-week parental leave is available for dads only and 90% of dads take advantage of the benefit.

By making it more acceptable for men to take time off and for women to pursue careers, we can change some of the unconscious biases and achieve not only equality, but a well-balanced and healthy society.

Many women of the baby boom generation are more open to this and think it's great that men are taking a more hands-on approach around the household. Men often joke and say that the younger generation is making them look bad.

---

8 https://www.nav.no/en/Home/Benefits+and+services

The next-generation of men understands true partnership. It doesn't matter who does what. We need to work together.

It's hard to believe in this day and age that societal pressures and unconscious biases still influence men and women into more traditional roles. It is changing, but not at a very fast pace. The more men take on domestic duties and women pursue careers, the sooner true equality will exist.

With the cost of living as high as it is in most major cities, it is a current reality that both men and women need to work to support a family.

With both partners working, it's no surprise that there aren't enough hours in the day to keep everything under control —both at home and in two workplaces. That's why so much has been written about Work/Life Balance.

WORK/LIFE BALANCE

Work/life balance is a hot topic, because we all seek it, but very few know how to achieve it, even though it's a function of common sense and instinct. We feel stressed and pulled into different directions. We believe we have no time or energy to address the imbalance so we end up living this frantic pace based on keeping every plate spinning like a carnival juggler.

Add to this a highly competitive social and professional culture that heaps enormous pressure on us to constantly rank and compare ourselves to others and devalues balance, and it becomes obvious why it is so easy to fall out of balance.

Don't get me wrong, competition is healthy and good for us and having role models to look up to is wonderful, but you need to have a solid relationship with yourself and value who you are in order to survive in this culture. You are unique with different capabilities, different work/life values. Knowing who you are and appreciating what you bring to the table will prevent you from trying to be someone you're not.

My sister and I are complete opposites. We are very close in age but could not be more different. I'm the academic, she is the creative. I am go-go-go, she prefers a leisurely pace. I'm an extrovert to the bone, she's more introverted. I am grateful we are different as we bring different things to the table for mutual benefit.

Introverts, by the way, may not be what you think they are. Introverts are misunderstood as antisocial wallflowers, but that is not the case at all. The difference between the two lies in what drains your energy and what you need to do to recharge your batteries.

- Extroverts re-energize by being around people. Being alone can be a drain on their energy banks.
- Introverts need time away from people to refill their energy banks.

I know introverts who can be the life of the party, give the most dynamic presentations, and who are super social. But when they are done, they're done. One is not better than the other. In fact, in life and in business, partnerships and teams perform better with a balance of the two. Go figure, there's that word 'balance' again.

Just figure out which one you are and make sure you get the time you need to recharge your batteries—whether it's with people or without.

I work long hours and I work hard during those hours. Recently my son asked me why I work so much and I said: 'because I love what I do'. His favorite activity is fishing. He has no trouble spending eight hours straight fishing. That's something I would hate (especially since I get sea sick).

What he loves sounds like work to me and what I love sounds like work to him. My point is that if you do what you love, it's not work and you won't think twice about doing it.

For some people working at 20 hours a week is maximum capacity, for others working 60 hours a week is normal.

I think people struggle with work/life balance because they don't like what they do for work or they have chosen a lifestyle that isn't really what they want.

For me, work/life balance means Monday to Friday I'm focused on my career. Evenings and weekends are family time. I take regular holidays and fit exercise into my weekly routine.

Sometimes I take on too many projects and I struggle to get everything done. When that happens, usually it's my family time that suffers and that's not okay. (Not completing projects is also not okay with me.)

I have physical symptoms when I'm getting out of balance: I get a lump in my throat that won't go away. Once I am aware of that lump, anxious thoughts get triggered. They sound like: 'I have so much to do, where do I start?', 'I've got so many deadlines, how am I going to get it all done?', 'Have I bitten off more than I can chew?' or 'Am I able to deliver on a promise I made to the level I want to deliver on?'

On the family front, I start thinking: 'I haven't spent enough time with my husband, will this jeopardize our marriage?' or 'How am I going to get my son to his sporting events when they clash with my schedule. How do I choose? What if I choose wrong?'

I set high expectations for myself which can be a double-edged sword: it drives me and pushes me forward, but sometimes, those expectations make me take on a superhuman amount of work. Somehow it always gets done.

Whenever I find myself over-committed, I get pragmatic about what needs to get done. I do a work/life triage assessment to identify priorities and the shortest, most professional route back to balance. I apologize to my family and assure them I am doing everything I can to get back on track.

Nobody can do it all. It comes down to prioritizing what's most important and recognizing what's realistic.

It's difficult to say 'no' sometimes as there are so many things I want to do.

It is no one else's job to decide what your balance should look like. Everyone has a different idea of what balance is and you cannot compare your life to someone else's in determining what's right for you. We all have to invest the time to figure it out. Staying in balance is a work in progress.

When you've got it right, you feel happy. You feel at ease and at peace and ready to realize your goals and dreams.

THE LIFE WHEEL

I categorize all the different aspects of my life and I put them into something I call the 'Life Wheel'. Visualize a classic pie chart and slice it up into many different pieces: career, family, health and fitness, friendships, romance, creative endeavours, finances, education, travel, entertainment, spirituality…the categories are yours to create.

The 'Perfect' Life Wheel Balance

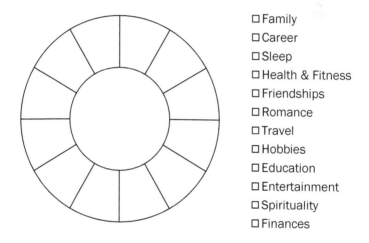

□ Family
□ Career
□ Sleep
□ Health & Fitness
□ Friendships
□ Romance
□ Travel
□ Hobbies
□ Education
□ Entertainment
□ Spirituality
□ Finances

Now that you've figured out what's important to you, shade in each block to the level of your satisfaction with it. If you're fully satisfied, you can shade the segment in fully. If you're totally unsatisfied, leave it white. And of course, any amount of shading in between is up to you. You could choose to make personal priorities one colour and career priorities a different colour. Or you can create a kaleidoscope of colour.

No matter how you colour it, you'll start to see a picture arise. Most notably, there are some areas that you're not quite as satisfied with as you could be or would like to be.

It's time for a priority check. Are the things you are not satisfied with things that are truly important to you? If you had an extra hour available to you each day (ie, 25 hours a day instead of 24) would you allocate it to any of those 'less-than-satisfied' areas? If not, maybe it's not that important a priority, or maybe it's a priority you feel you 'should have', as opposed to a priority you really want for yourself.

Once you get to a realistic picture of your priorities and your current satisfaction levels, you'll be ready to figure out how you can improve those areas.

Let's look at the gaps in your Life Wheel that prevent it from looking like a fully functioning wheel —or a kaleidoscope, if you've gone the colourful route. Seeing is believing and once the evidence is in front of you, you are empowered to do something about it.

A perfect balance ultimately would be fully shaded all the way around to create a perfect wheel. When everything is in alignment, the wheel rolls smoothly. If you have pockets of air in any one of those areas—maybe you only give yourself a 5 in intimate relationships and 6 in finance—your wheel is not smooth. It's wobbly, it clunks along, and if it stays out of alignment for too long, it starts negatively impacting the other areas of the wheel.

If your spine is out of alignment, it will show up somewhere in your body in the form of discomfort or pain. If you don't get it fixed it will start impacting other parts of your body. All of a sudden your hip might hurt, then maybe your knee. Perhaps you'll start to get headaches. It's all connected. When one part of your body is out of alignment, other parts compensate. It takes self-awareness to recognize the symptoms and take action. It's not always easy to notice when something's wrong. This is as true for how we live our lives as it is in our bodies.

On the other hand, when things are going really well, wow! The opposite happens and it compounds in a positive way. You'll be more productive, energetic and happier. What happens when you're happy? You have more energy, you get more done, and the cycle continues. You feel that you can accomplish anything you want. You feel in control and in sync with what is going on.

The old 'out of sight out of mind' adage might help you cope in the short term, but it just compounds the problem and lies waiting to blow up in your face one day.

Let's talk about the gaps. What can you do to get your house in order again? Acknowledging the issue and asking yourself what you can do to put it back in order is step one.

Fitting everything in is a challenge, but I don't subscribe to the 'I don't have time' excuse as it's not really true.

We all have the same 24 hours in a day. Sleep should take a full third of your time (33%). Work should take about 25% of your time. Add some time each week to get to and from work — say about 3% if you take 30 minutes each way. That's 60% of your life taken up by necessities. But it leaves 40% of your time to dedicate to everything else that's important to you.

That's at least 65 hours a week free to take care of your health, fitness, family, relationships and anything else that will balance your Life Wheel. It's about the choices we make.

How will you spend that 65 hours? Make yourself another chart you might call 'the Time Budget'. Again, the categories are yours to invent. Everyone's life is different. How much time do you spend in a typical week on exercise? On family time? On domestic chores like cooking, cleaning or taking the car to the garage for service? Hanging with friends? You've got at least 65 hours to allocate.

The Time Budget

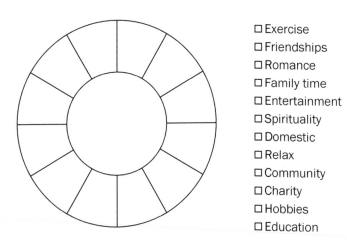

☐ Exercise
☐ Friendships
☐ Romance
☐ Family time
☐ Entertainment
☐ Spirituality
☐ Domestic
☐ Relax
☐ Community
☐ Charity
☐ Hobbies
☐ Education

Now that you've allocated where the time goes, think back to your Life Wheel.

Are there things you're spending your time on that aren't contributing to your priorities? How much time are you spending on tv? On Youtube? Facebook? Can you cut back so you can dedicate that time to something more important?

Look at ways to 'double dip' as I like to call it. My son has to be at his lacrosse games an hour before game time. I often use that hour to fit in a workout, catch up on personal emails and bill payments or socialize with friends. Or even better, I'll workout with a friend so I can socialize and fit in exercise at the same time. Then I watch the game. Triple dip!

When my husband and I go to charity fundraising dinners, we make sure to go with one or two other couples. It checks off three boxes for us: intimate relationships, friendships and philanthropy.

Did you know that most gyms have televisions in the cardio equipment? You could be working out while you're catching up on your favorite show. Or you could use your online time to catch up with friends on Skype or Facetime.

When you start to consider the time you spend 'on idle' instead of working on a priority, you'll be in a better position to make choices about how you spend your day and budget your time.

 *Ever wonder why some people seem to have so much energy and never appear stressed? The answer is simple. They sleep well, eat well, exercise and have purpose.*

Sleep Well

The average person needs seven to nine hours of sleep each and every night.[9] That doesn't mean you can't get less and still make it through your day, but it is very likely that you won't be nearly as productive as you could be. Robbing yourself of sleep because you're busy is not sustainable over the long run. Making sleep a priority will ensure you can perform.

If you find you just don't have enough hours in the day to get everything done and still get a good night's sleep, it's time to seriously look at your commitments and eliminate something. Are you truly focused during the day on tackling your priorities? Or are you easily distracted by things that suck up your time? Do you have trouble saying no? Trouble delegating? Calendaring?

If you have trouble falling asleep or staying asleep through the night, keep a pad of paper and a pen beside your bed.

If you can't fall asleep because things are still on your mind, write them down. If you wake up in the middle of the night because you're thinking about something, write it down. The brain is a fantastic processing unit, but a lousy storage device. If you're worried you're going to forget something, write it down. The process of writing things down allows your brain to relax as it no longer has to work to remember. This in turn allows your body to relax and fall asleep.

In order to fall asleep, I need to clear my mind. I need to do what I like to call a brain-dump. Once I've written my thoughts down, I have the freedom to sleep without worrying about yesterday… or worrying about tomorrow.

---

9 http://sleepfoundation.org/how-sleep-works/

Before you fall asleep at night, write down a list of your top three accomplishments for the day. Maybe you made it to the gym, even though you thought you were too tired. Maybe you read your child a long bedtime story. Maybe you said no to dessert. Praise yourself for progress on your priorities. It doesn't matter how big or small the accomplishments were, the process of identifying them requires you to process your entire day. Processing your entire day helps you to think about tomorrow and next steps. While you're at it, write down your top three goals for tomorrow.

Have a hot bath before bed. Heat relaxes your muscles and sends signals to the brain that it's time to relax and unwind. Take some deep breaths and let the tension go.

After a hot bath, put on comfortable pajamas and stretch for 10 minutes. Your muscles are already warm, so it's easier to stretch. As you stretch, continue to take deep breaths and focus on letting go of stress. Crawl into bed and be prepared to fall into a deep sleep.

Be careful not to re-stimulate the brain after you've completed your list and your bath. It's not a good idea to have a television in the bedroom; it causes the brain to awaken rather than relax.

I often read before bed as it helps me transition from one train of thought to another, and then I can fall asleep. I need to be careful what book I'm reading otherwise it will have the reverse effect. Educational books are a no-no for me before bed as they simply get my brain focused back on what I did all day and give me new ideas for tomorrow. I need to start the entire relaxation process over again. A good novel will send my mind into more of a dream-like state, which is great for falling asleep. If I'm engrossed in a really good page-turner, I make sure I go to bed an hour earlier to allow enough time to read before I fall asleep and still ensure I get at least eight hours sleep a night.

I used to work with a woman who claimed she only needed five or six hours of sleep every night. She had a busy life outside of work as she juggled five kids and everything that goes along with running a household. She was disciplined enough to get herself up early in the mornings to fit in exercise before making everyone's lunches, paying bills and getting ready for work herself.

But guess what? She needs more sleep than she thinks. She may go through all the motions in a day, but she is not producing at an optimal level. In meetings she can barely keep her eyes open. As long as the tasks she's given are basic with clear instructions she can get them done, but don't expect her to problem solve as her brain just isn't operating at that level.

Eat Well

To keep our bodies healthy, we need to ensure we get our daily requirement of healthy foods: a balance of proteins, healthy fats and energy producing carbohydrates. Eating right not only prevents us from getting sick, but it gives us the energy we need to perform at our peak.

We all know we should eat well, so why is it difficult? Busy schedules often cause us to grab a bite on the run. Planning in advance and ensuring healthy snacks are readily available will help prevent a fast food encounter.

Moods affect cravings, so pay close attention to your personal trigger points. When you're feeling blue and craving ice cream, try going for a brisk walk, or brush your teeth. Exercise has a positive effect on moods and can help curb cravings.

Keep some low calorie ice cream bars on hand in case you still need a little something. The old saying 'everything in moderation' is a good principle to live by.

A tool I use from time to time when I need a little motivation to clean up my eating habits, is the 'Fitbit' app at www.fitbit.com. You can download it to your phone for easy access to track calories, exercise, weight and water consumption. It allows you to set goals and track your progress. By inputting everything you consume, it creates an awareness which shifts behavior and the result is healthier food choices ... which leads to a healthier you.

Exercise

Some people use meditation or regular 10 minute stretch breaks—you will know what works for you best—but clearing the mind and connecting with the body works for everyone.

I use exercise. It does double duty—a stress reliever and energy source. I don't have endless energy or time, but I have a commitment to a healthy balanced life.

Positive energy equals success, and working out gives me positive energy. It clears my mind; it puts my priorities in order.

If I have a stressful day where it seems like the only solution is to work until 10 pm to get it all done, I book myself a personal training session. I make the commitment and I go—even when I have to borrow time from something else to get there. I get to the gym and—all of a sudden—work is a hundred miles away. When I get back, what I thought was going to take me 4 hours to do, can be whipped off in less than an hour. It usually turns out that it wasn't such a big deal. It was just my mind needing a rest.

When you feel overwhelmed, it's easy to make mountains out of molehills. You need to take a break and relieve stress.

I was asked once: Have you ever regretted working out? No. Never. Not once. Have I ever regretted not going? Usually. Yes. Most the time.

If you know you should have done something you didn't do, you often regret it. As I said earlier, setting attainable goals does a lot for building confidence. If you make little promises to yourself and you don't stick to them, you've let yourself down. End of story.

 *If you make a promise to yourself, stick to it.*

Regular exercise can extend life expectancy and greatly improve the quality of life. Our bodies are designed to move and need regular activity to function properly.

Making exercise a priority will help improve every other aspect of your life. Studies show that exercise controls weight, combats diseases and health conditions, aids with sleep, fights depression, improves moods and energy levels, decreases stress and increases your productivity. I think most of us can agree that exercise is important, yet many struggle with making it a priority.

The key is to find activities that you enjoy, whether it's a brisk walk, a fitness class, yoga, running, biking, aerobics, weight-lifting, rowing or a dance class. There are a million different activities to get the body moving to improve your health, and variety is great in keeping you interested and motivated.

I find it best to block the time in my calendar so I have a good chance of sticking to my commitment. Booking a workout with a trainer or a friend is an added insurance policy that I won't back out. I've experienced many days where I would have skipped exercising had it not been for a fitness 'appointment'.

It's easy to forget to put yourself first, but if you don't take care of yourself, you're no good to anyone else.

Purpose

For the majority of the population, work is just a way to pay the bills. Working to live versus living to work. And that's sad. When I ask people about retirement, I can tell who loves their job. Those who can't wait to retire don't love what they do.

I don't see myself retiring. Why would I retire? I love what I do and I get paid for it. I see myself always doing something I love and likely getting paid to do it

If you find yourself stressed when you go into the office, or find fitting everything in is difficult to do and it overwhelms you, check your Life Wheel. You're probably out of balance.

When talking to university students, I am blown away by the number of young women whose top priority is centered on having a work/life balance. They don't even have a job yet! Or a partner, or kids! Wow! Put the brakes on. Stop worrying so much about the work/life balance and just deal with it as it comes.

It's great to set goals and figure out what you want to do, but you won't know what your own work/life balance looks like until you start really living it.

If someone told me when I was in university that I would work 50-60 hours per week, be a mother, wouldn't take maternity leave and would go into debt to start my career, I would have stressed about work/life balance and maybe not jumped into this life quite so wholeheartedly as I did.

What I had yet to learn was that work doesn't have to be 'work' and neither should it be seen as what stands between you and retirement or the 'good life'. You can think of work as how you are contributing to society. You can enjoy what you do and cultivate a sense of purpose.

Find a career path that allows you to help others, allows you to contribute to society, gives you a sense of accomplishment, and you'll quickly find that you're enjoying it. It won't feel like work at all. To me that's the kind of purpose we are all meant to know.

 *The short lesson is: start by believing you can have a job that you enjoy.*

EFFECTIVENESS

I am constantly recalibrating my Life Wheel to be fully in the game, to stay balanced and therefore able to give 100%. The success I experience is directly proportionate to the caliber of focus and effort I bring to the table. Execution is key. Education and training are important, but it's how you convert that knowledge and experience into action that really matters.

There are a number of reasons why the failure rate in the finance industry is so high, but I see the number one reason as an inability to attract clients. Sometimes it's a lack of confidence. Sometimes it's a weakness in one's ability to market their skills. But I think if you dig a bit deeper, the real reason people fail to attract clients is a lack of effort.

People tend to be better at talking than doing. It's the doing that matters.

When you look at your Life Wheel, are your actions matching your priorities? If you want to grow your business, are you doing the right things to get the results you're looking for? Or are you making excuses and wasting time in other areas that are not a priority?

A fantastic book to read for further learning on this topic is '7 Habits of Highly Effective People' by Stephen Covey.

Sometimes women use family as an excuse to not go for the brass ring. Some women haven't figured out what it is they want to do. Sometimes women are too afraid to take that leap of faith into the right career path. Social pressures affect women's upward mobility—pressure to be the world's best mom AND have interesting, rewarding careers. Those two worlds are not compatible; they are adversarial in our society.

We women worry about what people think if we are career driven yet want to have a family. And we worry about being relegated to society's sidelines if we want to stay at home and raise our children.

Women need to check in with their goals, desires, dreams and take responsibility for the lives we are leading and the examples we are setting.

Blaming anyone or anything else for why we aren't successful is the ultimate indicator that we have abdicated our personal responsibility for our lives and our decisions.

A soon as you catch yourself blaming someone/something else for what's not working in your life and why your Life Wheel is out of whack, STOP IMMEDIATELY.

Ask yourself what you can do differently to change the outcome, because you only have control over what you do.

You cannot control the weather, other people, the economy... so the old saying of 'focus on what you can control and ignore the rest' proves true.

There are some cases where you do have some influence over others. You can persuade others to do things differently, but again, you can't control the outcome. What you can control is how you interact with someone to get a different response.

If you're unhappy with a situation, let's say an employee who is under-performing, you have to be aware of what drives that employee's behavior. You can control how you deal with it to get your desired outcome. If that employee functions best when you tell them what to do, you need to be direct and say what you expect and define what the employee needs to do and by when. If it's an employee who doesn't like confrontation and needs constant praise, you can take a softer approach to get the desired outcome or else they're going to buckle.

Three things hold us back in life: fear of mistakes, fear of change and pursuit of perfection.

Fear of Change

We can fall out of balance when we stay in roles because we become lazy and/or scared to make a change. How many times have you heard someone say 'the devil you know, is better than the devil you don't?' Well, guess what.

 *The devil is not in the unknown; it's in our fears and our limiting beliefs.*

What I hear often from people who are considering a career in the financial industry is that they're scared because the first few years are tough and the failure rate is very high. They don't want to take the chance because it's a big leap at the beginning. They dwell on the negative aspects by over thinking the potential failures.

As I shared earlier, my husband and I agreed to risk a year supplementing his income from our line of credit while I worked to build my business. I didn't ignore the risks that year presented—I faced them head on and made a plan for navigating them.

I have a track record which told me two things and gave me the confidence to jump into the deep end:

- I win way more than I don't.
- Effort equals results.

Fear of Failure

We all fall into the trap of trying to have everything figured out before we attempt something new or different.

This is a huge mistake. Often by the time we have it figured out, the opportunity is long gone. As great as it is to have a very clear end goal, it's not always realistic. Sometimes you just need to start walking down the path and let it unfold as you go along. Sitting paralyzed in planning until you figure it out isn't going to get you anywhere. There's nothing wrong with changing direction if opportunities arise or circumstances change.

If fear of failure is holding you back, get over it (it seems I have said this before).

A small element of risk-taking is a necessary ingredient in everything that we do. We are okay with taking risks when it's something relatively benign like a new haircut or adopting a dog, but when it involves money, our careers, or our heart's deepest desire, we tend to back away from the edge of risk like it's a mile-high cliff we're peering over. We sit down, get out the map, the climbing manual, check the weather report and wait for that perfect opportunity or some kind of sign that it's time to step over the edge.

I don't beat myself up if I don't do exactly what I set out to do. I won't succeed at everything I try. It's okay to fail. It's okay to make mistakes. I'm prepared to accept that not every decision I make is going to be the right one. I run on faith that most of decisions I make are the right ones for me. I strive for perfection, but not to the point where it limits my productivity.

About 5 years into building my business, I decided I needed to hire someone in order to help me take my business to the next level. I wanted someone with experience to handle some of my client relationships, help bring in new clients and assist with taking care of my up-island clients so I wouldn't have to travel as often.

I found the perfect candidate: a woman with close to 20 years' experience in the business (primarily in support roles) who had recently started building her own business as a financial advisor. She was struggling to get traction in growing the assets under her management. Since I had a proven strength in her weak area, I thought I could mentor her in that area while she would support me where I needed help.

She was extremely professional, appeared confident, dressed great and said all the right things. Since she was older and more experienced than I was, I set up a high compensation package and treated her like a business partner. I paid her a hefty salary plus a generous percent of the revenue we generated.

She wasn't as strong a candidate as I had thought. She continued to struggle with bringing in new assets, second-guessed herself and lacked some critical knowledge that was surprising given her tenure in the industry. She was a hard worker but she wasn't a smart worker. She ended up spending a considerable amount of time on unproductive activities—spinning her wheels.

I had put myself into a position of having an assistant who was earning partner-level compensation. I tried to mentor and train her to the role I hired her for, but ultimately had to let her go. It was a costly mistake. Not only had I overpaid her during the time she worked for me, I had to offer a severance package.

In hindsight, I should have asked her tougher questions in the interview stage. I didn't do enough due diligence before pulling the trigger and paid for it.

That said, I tried and learned from my mistakes. I failed, but I survived and moved on.

Pursuit of Perfection

When I was trying to get into business school, grades mattered, so I put in the hours I needed to get accepted into the program. Once I was in, I knew I had the ability to get the straight A's, but I made a conscious decision not to set that as a goal. The difference in time commitment between getting an A+ and B+ was huge. The B's came easy, but to get straight A's would have required an extra fifteen to twenty hours a week of study time. I asked myself if it was worth it, and concluded it wasn't. I was able to channel those extra twenty hours a week working to gain practical experience instead. I believe that work experience had a far greater positive impact on my career than straight As would have.

The money I earned from working allowed me to cover university expenses and reduced financial stress, which helped further balance my wheel. I graduated with a decent GPA, but nobody in the real world asked me about it as grades don't seem to be part of the decision making process for employers. I don't ask to see grades when I interview candidates for a job. Grades don't tell the whole story and in some cases, they can be misleading. Some people are book-smart but street-stupid. In the real world, being street-smart is often more valuable. When you find people who have both smarts, you've got it made.

 *We have more control over our success than we give ourselves credit for.*

YOUR FINANCES

Since I make a living counselling people about building wealth, I can't help but slip in a small chapter on what to do if you're less than satisfied with the "Finances" section of your Life Wheel. Maybe you don't have enough money to do the things you want to do in your life, or you're struggling to pay your bills.

When people feel stressed about money, they're usually spending more than they are earning. It's that simple! Of course life can throw us curveballs that knock us off balance, like losing a job or facing an unexpected major expense, but our reaction to any unfortunate situation will determine the outcome. In its simplest form, there are really only three ways to fix a cash flow problem:

- Earn more money. Maybe it's a career change, a second job, or asking your boss for a raise.
- Spend less. Take ownership of current spending patterns and look for things to cut down or cut out.
- A combination of both.

No amount of complaining will solve the problem. Excuses like 'I don't get paid enough' … 'the cost of living has gone through the roof' … 'the government should reduce our taxes' may all be true, but the real stress comes from allowing outside circumstances to control what your financial situation looks like.

 *Blaming others for the situation you find yourself in is a powerless place to be. But you can change it.*

First you have to recognize that you've made a bad decision and that no one else is at the helm of your life. You have control. You always have had control. If you gave it away, take it back and start to make new, better decisions. Change your direction. If you need help, get it from the right people who will listen to what you want and need. Don't look back.

Taking care of your financial well-being, is more than just about earning and spending. It's also about having your eye on the big picture. Once you've gotten your spending in line with your earning (or your earning in line with your spending), there are four other major steps in getting the "Finances" section of your Life Wheel into balance, otherwise the problems will continue to come back, and the price tag will get bigger and bigger.

Calculate your net worth.

Put together a list of all your assets (ie. investment accounts, savings, house, etc). Next put together a list of your liabilities (credit card balances, mortgage balance, line of credit, etc). When listing your liabilities, you want to put down the total amount owing, not your monthly payments as that should be listed above under cash flow. Subtract your total liabilities from your total assets and you have your net worth. This number is meaningless without knowing what you need it for, which takes us to setting financial goals.

What do you want to accomplish?

Think big! If you don't set a goal, you are unlikely to achieve it. Most people want to pay off debt and save for the future, which is great, but I suggest being more specific. If retirement is your goal, you need to decide at what age and how much income per year do you want. You can work with a financial planner or advisor to help brainstorm goals and build a plan to achieve the specific goals you desire.

Invest Wisely

Do you know what your investment options are? There is a big difference between GICs and stocks, mutual funds and exchange traded funds (ETFs). There are pros and cons to each type of investment, not to mention varying levels of risk and opportunity. Take the time to learn the basics so you can make better investment decisions and understand how those decisions impact your life goals. For example, a GIC is safe as your capital is guaranteed, but the interest rate is extremely low and doesn't keep up with taxes and inflation, so will do little to help you achieve your long term goals. Stocks come in many different risk categories, don't offer guarantees, but do have higher return potential than GICs and provide a better chance of achieving long term goals.

Protect your family

Have you planned for the unexpected? What would the impact be if you were unable to work? What if you were no longer here at all? Would there be a burden left behind or have you put a plan in place to take care of loved ones? Will the tax man be the beneficiary of your estate? It's important to look at the impact of potential scenarios to ensure you can protect your family.

If you've been putting off taking these steps because it sounds complicated, get over it and get on with it. There's an entire industry full of professionals who are ready to help. You don't have to go it alone. The moment you've tackled this, you'll feel more in control of your financial situation. Stress reduced. Balance restored.

HAVING IT ALL

Let's talk about retirement. Your retirement party happened a month ago. You wake up. It's Monday morning. It's winter. What are you going to do today? Tomorrow? Next week? What do you want to do?

People stumble when asked these questions. They have a hard time conceptualizing how they will fill their days because they think in generic terms: Golf. Travel. Spend time with the grandchildren.

Don't defer pleasure, work it in now. If you want to golf, fit golf into your schedule even if it's a juggle sometimes. You can always golf more later on, but if you have nothing but time to golf, it is going to get very boring. Even golf fanatics do not want to golf every day, eight hours a day, seven days a week.

There are other things to do with life, so figure out what it is that you are enjoy doing and get out there and do it. Chase fulfillment and it will come.

Let's take travel as an example. I want to travel and see the world so I'm doing that now. I take holidays and do the things I want to do, I don't want to wait until retirement; I do it now.

 *You can have it all, but having it all might not mean what you thought it was.*

Make a plan and get started. Don't worry that your plan isn't perfect. It never is. You'll need to be prepared to change directions as you discover things you didn't realize before, things you never thought of before and directions you never imagined you would go.

Don't overthink it and make it more complicated than it needs to be. Keep it simple; make it a fun exercise.

Seek challenge. Make decisions based on what you enjoy doing. You'll be able to fit it all in. You will, trust me; it will work.

Success is not about the size of your paycheque or dollars in the bank. Those are the wrong measuring sticks. What good is it to have millions of dollars in the bank if you're not enjoying it or doing anything with it?

Imagine this: an entrepreneur on vacation in Mexico sees a fisherman going out in the morning to fish. The fisherman brings back four or five fish to feed his family, and the entrepreneur says, 'Hey, if you bought four more boats, you'll be able to bring in forty fish and you could sell them to restaurants and make lots of money. You could buy more boats and make even more money.' The fisherman says, 'But then what do I do?' The entrepreneur assures him that he can build a huge company, get wealthy, sell it and retire. The fisherman responds, 'Then what do I do?' The entrepreneur says, 'You can come here on vacation and fish' and the fisherman answers, 'But that's what I'm already doing.'

A study[10] by Princeton University shows that once your income is over $75,000 per year (as of 2010), making more money doesn't make you happier.

10http://content.time.com/time/magazine/article/0,9171,2019628,00.html

Whatever the correct amount is, the point of the statement is that once you've covered life's necessities, making more money won't have the same impact.

People are driven by different desires and feel pulled in different directions. People driven by greed and the desire to make money, for the sake of making money, will never be happy. They will never have enough. When people make more money they spend more money. Funny how that works. As they do this, they have to work harder and life gets busier and more complicated. Meanwhile their stress levels go up and work/life balance gets out of whack. As we think about the fisherman story I just told, he was already living the life he wanted. Making more money would only complicate things and eventually bring him back to where he was already happy.

Make sure you're not wasting time on things that don't matter, and make sure the things that matter are at the top your list.

In order to ensure you're doing this, you have to have goals and you need to know how you want your Life Wheel to look. You must define what's important to you and how much time should you be spending in each of those areas to be happy.

From a business perspective, what is your business plan? What do you need to do? What are your goals for your business or your career? What do you need to do to achieve them?

What are your aspirations? What do you need to do to get to where you want to go? If it's to climb the corporate ladder, what do you need to do to get recognized and to be skilled and capable of achieving that? Maybe it's taking some courses, maybe it's attending presentations.

Whatever it is, you have to set goals; you have a look at every task you're doing, and assess how these tasks fit with your life goals, your career aspirations or your business plan, your lifestyle, and your Life Wheel. If they fit, do it. If they don't fit, it's a distraction. Don't do it! This is easier said than done, and it's not a one-time exercise, it requires continuous review.

The person who constantly seems frazzled and in panic mode trying to get everything done has most likely not prioritized and therefore taken on too much.

 *Life doesn't have to be as complicated as we make it.*

I learned the hard way a number of years ago that when I am operating at full capacity and something unexpected comes along, I'm in trouble. It may be an illness, an accident or a crisis of some sort. It doesn't matter what it is. In order to create the time to handle the situation, something else has to go. Re-prioritizing must take place. There are some things that should always be a priority no matter what: eight hours sleep every night, healthy eating and regular exercise. If you don't take care of your health first, nothing else will matter if you end up sick or dead.

It is very easy to get distracted each and every day with things that don't matter. Just look at how many things come in your email inbox. In today's world we are inundated and can get easily distracted. I don't have time to read everything that comes in my inbox, so I have to be strategic about it. Delete is my favorite button. Unsubscribe is even better.

Questions to ask yourself regularly: 'What are my priorities for the day, the week, the month, the quarter, the year? Do these activities fit with my larger goals and priorities?'

 *Be flexible and understand that priorities may change or other opportunities may come along.*

That being said, don't use 'opportunity' as an excuse to get distracted by whatever is new and shiny this week and risk not accomplishing anything.

For example: you set a goal to grow your business by 20% percent and you've got a game plan on what that's going to look like. Meanwhile, a new opportunity comes up that actually could increase your business by 50% percent, but you turn it down because it would take you a different direction than your original game plan. Well, that's just... not smart. Be focused but not rigid, and be adaptable and flexible enough to shift along the way.

Conversely, if an opportunity is pulling you away from what you know you need to get done now , turn it down. Get good at saying 'not right now'.

Essential to our work/life balance is confidence. Too many of us subscribe to this idea that we have to be perfect, that we have to have every answer and that only when we are perfect and in command of every unknown, will we be confident enough to step out and take a chance on something new.

We worry about whether we know enough, we doubt our capabilities. We take on more than we should to prove we are just as good as the men who work less. We overwhelm ourselves with information before we take action.

I have a female colleague who regularly second-guesses herself and over-analyzes things. She is plagued by self-doubt and low self-esteem, yet is amazingly bright and would rank amongst the top quartile of advisors in the company in the smarts department.

She is a sponge for new information as she wants to be an expert to feel better about herself. The problem is, she has trouble retaining it all because she's spending so much time reading articles that she's not slowing down to absorb the information or place it in context. She puts pressure on herself to know the answer to everything that might be asked of her. She doesn't realize this is an impossible quest. It's okay to not know all the answers as long as you know where to find them.

I catch her putting herself down saying things like 'I know this is a stupid question, but…' or, 'I know I'm not as smart as you.' That's what she's saying out loud; I can only imagine how negative her own self-talk is.

What she doesn't realize is that by making these statements out loud, others perceive her as lacking confidence and are less likely to promote her or give her new business.

She wasn't even aware that she was putting herself down and wasting time on non-productive activities until I shared my observations. Bringing awareness helped change her behaviour and her confidence has improved.

I've even caught myself at various stages in my career, taking on way too much to ensure I am perceived by my male colleagues as a strong leader and a valuable contributor. I get addicted to the fast pace and delivery of results. Sometimes I burn myself out so my family gets the exhausted version of me. That's not fair to them or to me.

PRODUCTIVITY TRIAGE

In all of my practice for work/life balance, time management, and prioritizing tasks, I developed an approach to help me stay focused on the right things. I call this the 'QUICK plan to productivity'

Q   **Quit** = Stop wasting time doing things that don't matter.

U   **Unload** = Delegate to someone else.

I   **Immediate** = Do it immediately, stop procrastinating

C   **Calendar** = Schedule a task for a later date so it's off your mind, but doesn't get forgotten.

K   **Keep** = File for later reference, but do not hoard.

Quit

We live in a world of information overload and it is easy to hold onto way too much stuff! Think of all the junk emails you receive on a regular basis, or the amount of hard copy reading material you bring home from a conference. Get rid of most, if not all, of it. Why are you saving things that you are highly unlikely to ever read again? Eliminate as much as possible of the things you don't need. Unsubscribe from as many email lists as you possibly can to reduce the constant inflow of information that serves no purpose. Take a moment to think about every piece of information you are given and decide what's important and what's not (or not right now). It will feel like a load was lifted and will free up your head to think clearly. In an extreme example, think of a hoarder. What judgements do you make of that person? Do you have a tiny bit of hoarder behavior too?

In addition to getting rid of the stuff that doesn't matter, Quit means to quit doing things that don't matter. Watch how you spend your time and ask yourself if your actions align with your priorities. It's too easy to get caught up in activities that don't add value and, in fact, negatively impact other aspects of our lives.

A friend of mine often complains about not having enough time to spend with her daughter, yet will spend three hours at the bar with co-workers Friday afternoon or get sucked into spending a day at a conference on a topic that doesn't directly relate to her key priorities. I understand it's easy to get swept up in the moment, but bringing awareness to this and reminding ourselves of what's really important can greatly assist with time management and ultimately achieving a truly well balanced life.

Complaining about things while making no effort to change them will lead to a high-stress, high-anxiety lifestyle.

Unload

You can't do it all! If you are in a management or leadership position with people that report to you, review the tasks you have on your plate and consider what you can delegate to someone else to complete. You should be spending your time doing the things that can only be done by you. If someone else can help, take advantage of that. I don't mean to dump your work onto someone else and not do anything yourself, but I do mean delegate the tasks that you should be delegating. I struggled with this for many years earlier in my career, and still catch myself struggling from time to time as I know I can do the task and don't want to inconvenience others. Sometimes it's just quicker to do it yourself, but that is a dangerous place to be as we run out of time to do it all. How will others learn and develop new skills if never given the opportunity to try?

Unloading applies in non-work situations as well. Think about all the tasks that need to get done at home. Who does the dishes, cleans the house, makes dinner, schedules parent teacher interviews, mows the lawn, plans family vacations? In a family situation, these tasks should get distributed among family members. Children can start making their own lunches and clean their rooms at a young age. Not only will that help with time management, but it is an important life skill and will build confidence and a sense of independence. As kids get older, they can start mowing the lawn, doing the dishes, washing their own laundry and helping cook dinner. Spouses should be a team and equally contribute to the family enterprise. Each member of the family plays an important role, and working together as a team will benefit all.

Immediate Action

Putting things off that should get done now creates a backlog of work that will nag at you, affect your energy level and erode confidence. We tend to procrastinate on things we don't really enjoy doing, yet often feel really good once those things are done. It's about doing what you said you were going to do. If you have an appointment booked, or a task scheduled that needs attention today, don't defer or cancel without a very good reason.

Before taking immediate action, however, ensure that the task at hand is important (versus not relevant to your priorities and therefore 'Quit'), ensure it can't be done by someone else ('Unload'), and it shouldn't be pushed out on your calendar to get completed at a later date (see calendar).

Calendar

Calendar is about blocking time on your calendar and scheduling tasks. I am a list person and find that writing things down helps me stay focused and productive. It takes the pressure off my brain (memory) so I can think more clearly and perform at my best. Every day I review my schedule and task list to prioritize my day and get as much done as possible. I try to schedule the task for the specific date it needs to get done as opposed to just having one giant task list that I'm constantly working from.

If I am scheduled to deliver a presentation in three months, I calculate how much prep time I will need and schedule the time to prep the week before the presentation (or earlier as needed). This isn't procrastinating, it's prioritizing my time and freeing up my head-space so I don't keep thinking about it. It's not possible to get everything done at once, which is why prioritization is critical. When that day and time comes to do my preparation, I take immediate action to get it done.

Sometimes daily tasks or appointments I've scheduled no longer align with my key priorities. I either delete them altogether or delegate them to someone else if appropriate. It's much more efficient to not add the task or appointment in the first place, which requires a steady discipline of saying no to the things that aren't truly a fit. This is definitely easier than it sounds and requires practice and constant reminders. I find it helpful to have my key priorities written and visible at my desk at all times to serve as my reminder. My assistant is a great gatekeeper and resource and she will often question some of the things I say yes to, and keep me on track. My husband is great at spotting when I've over committed and reminds me to slow down and re-align my priorities. He gives me a lot of room to move and is extremely supportive, so I know to listen when he occasionally tells me I'm doing too much, as he is usually right.

Keep

There are always priorities that you can see in the distance heading your way. But if there isn't something you can do about it today, file it forward. Diarize it for another day. Don't get caught worrying about something that 'isn't today's problem'. Tackle today's problems today. Leave tomorrow's until tomorrow.

Take a look at what you're keeping and ask yourself why. Like purging your wardrobe or recycling old magazines and newspapers; let them go. Be purposeful about what you keep. Be mindful about what you discard.

Keep also refers to things that you know you will need to hold onto for future reference. The key here is to truly only keep what you really will need and can't locate elsewhere (ie. look up on the internet). For the things you do need to keep, ensure you have an excellent filing system to keep organized and easy to find when you need it. For example: you need to keep business receipts for tax purposes, so ensure you have a filing system to organize your receipts by year and by category / type that matches what the tax man is looking for. I have a file drawer that has different color folders for each type of record keeping. My home office expenses are in red folders, my rental property expenses are in blue folders, etc. Within each color system, I have sub categories for utilities, vehicle expense, income, repairs and maintenance and other applicable categories. At the end of the year when I'm preparing files for my accountant, everything is in order. I also use bookkeeping software so I can pull income and expense reports anytime I need them.

YOUR PROFESSIONAL NETWORK

Networking is about building relationships with people you can create win-win partnerships with.

In order for networking to be productive, it's important to be strategic and direct—to know what it is you hope to accomplish.

Prior to an event, find out who is going to be there, what opportunities the event presents, and determine what your desired outcome is. Adapt your intentions and expectations to suit the character of the event, but stay focused on how it fits with your objectives. Refine your questions and approach to make the most of these opportunities and to connect with dynamic people.

Networking can be the most powerful tool for building your business or advancing your career, or, done badly, can totally implode it.

There are three styles of networking that almost never work. Most of us avoid all three like the plague.

The used car salesman. That's the person who comes on too strong, too fast and is too much. We all know how it feels to be approached by this person.

The serial relationship builder. That's the other extreme — the person who spends so much time massaging the client with chit chat that they never get any business done. In other words, energy output does not get returned in business.

The wallflower. Those are the people who know that they need to go to events but they do no networking. They hope that just by showing up someone is going to notice them and the business is just going to come their way. A total waste of time.

When I started in financial services, my networking was largely trial and error because I didn't have a mentor to show me the way. All I knew was how I didn't want to come across: pushy, everyone's best friend, insincere or insecure.

I clearly remember my very first networking event. It was a local business mixer and I was simply directed to 'collect a bunch of business cards, follow up with people afterwards and get some business done'.

That approach didn't feel right for me as it seemed too 'salesy' and one sided, not mutually beneficial. I was concerned others would perceive me as desperate for business. I later learned the nickname awarded to this style of networking: Spray and Pray. Yuck, even the name is off-putting.

Spray and Pray is when you blast out a sales piece or a pitch to everyone and hope someone wants to do business with you. It's like dragnet fishing. You aim to catch a big fish by casting a huge net, but the reality is you'll also get seaweed, a bunch of small fish, some crab and even a bit of garbage. It's not an effective or a pleasant way to move around a room.

My impression of my first networking event was that it was a bunch of desperate and hungry business owners who were all trying to sell stuff to one another and didn't really care if it was a fit or not. Everybody talked, nobody listened. I felt awful. I left.

There had to be a better way to be out in the community building my business.

Networking is critical for a woman's career. Men have been doing it for years through their 'old boys clubs'. Many opportunities arise in business as a result of who you know, so women need to ensure they are known in their field if they want the same opportunities men have had. An advantage women have is that men typically want to talk to you! They may not feel comfortable leaving their cronies to kick-start a conversation, but I assure you that if a woman introduces herself to a group of men, it is very unlikely they would turn her away.

In the networking functions I have been to, my experience has been that women often fall into the role of the passive relationship builder. This is when women spend most of their time socializing and trying to make friends hoping that business will come eventually versus looking for mutually beneficial business opportunities now.

Being passive is waiting for things to happen; being active is making things happen.

It's great to have a conversation to figure out synergies and ask the right questions but at some point, you have to move on.

You've got to make 'The Ask'.

The Ask could sound like, 'I see some mutual synergies between the two of us. Can we book another time for you and I to just sit down and go through what that may look like? Yes?' Great. Take the card and move on to the next person.

If you're at a networking function and you want to work the room and meet as many people as you can, you have to go for it! It's like speed dating—you want to ask quick, pertinent questions that are going to get you the information you need, while still building a relationship and without appearing rushed.

To be able to move on, you can say, 'I could spend all night with you. I really feel a good synergy here. But there are a few other people that I would like to say hi to. Can I follow up with you another time?' You take the card and you move on because if you don't, the event will be over and you will have put all your eggs into one basket.

Women need to get over their fear of being perceived as too direct, which for men, seems to be a respected trait. People generally appreciate directness as long as the message is delivered in the right way—from a place of helpfulness, not rude or condescending.

 *Being direct is a much preferred approach over being passive aggressive or beating around the bush.*

I learned the hard way not to be a passive relationship builder. I was at a point in my career when I wanted to step into management. My branch manager was close to retirement, and I assumed I would be offered the role when the time came.

After all, I was the one who organized branch events, coordinated weekly sales meetings, and was the go-to person for information and problem solving.

Since I wanted to continue working with my clients while taking on the role of manager, I asked a colleague in the east how he managed to do both. The first thing out of his mouth was, 'Why do you ask, are you interested in becoming a branch manager? If so, you'd better put your hand up because they would never ask you.'

I was shocked! I couldn't figure out why they wouldn't ask me, but I learned it was partly due to an old boys club mentality and partly due to the fact that I hadn't demonstrated my skillset to the appropriate people or made it known that I wanted the job. In other words, I hadn't networked with the right people in the right way.

That was about to change. I immediately called the regional manager and said I was interested in becoming branch manager when the time came. He told me I'd have to talk the national manager into considering me. I spoke to the national manager who said I would have to talk the regional manager. Neither wanted to flat out say 'no' to me and were using each other as the out.

I didn't give up.

I continued to press and inquire about what it would take for them to give me a chance.

They asked me to complete a leadership skills assessment. I passed with flying colours.

They asked me to prepare a 3-year business plan to outline what value I could bring to the table and how that would help the firm and fit in with our strategic priorities. Nailed it.

They said they were interviewing two other candidates and would get back to me.

At the end of the day, I finally got the job but I was completely frustrated with the process, as no other manager in the country had gone through what I went through. I later learned that the reason they put me through the process was because I was a woman. Their unconscious biases couldn't see past my gender and it required me to prove myself before being considered. That was in 2010.

I am thankful that I was tipped off in advance to put my name in the hat for manager since I had not done as much as I could have to ensure I would see the opportunities I expected.

 *Short lesson: Networking within your organization is as critical to external networking to ensure opportunities will follow.*

When you're going to a networking event, make sure you have a goal in mind before you go in. What do you hope to accomplish? Who do you want to meet? Decide those things in advance so that you're not caught in idle chit chat about the weather or the hockey game.

Do you have a particular strategy when you're walking into a networking event? Do you hang around the front door? What part of the room do you gravitate to? I like to go straight to the bar because it is easy to strike up a conversation while people are waiting in line for a drink. It tends to be the most social spot, just like the kitchen at a house party.

I join into an existing conversation and have no problem doing it. Some people feel uncomfortable doing this as they don't want to interrupt, but I don't think it's rude, it's expected—we are all there to meet people.

Be aware of people's body language. If two people are really close together and it looks like they're having a serious conversation, don't drop in, let them finish their discussion. If you're not paying attention to body language you might get a dirty look if you try to jump into what is clearly a private conversation between two people.

But if you see a group of three or four people with space between them and their body language is open and inviting, join their circle. But listen first! Don't say anything right away. Stand tall and confident, don't shrink or keep your body small. Mirror the body language of those around you; keep it open and inviting. When they're finished or when there's a pause in the conversation, it's your cue to introduce yourself. Shake everyone's hands, get their names and either add a comment to their previous conversation if appropriate or start a new topic with a thought-provoking question.

Most women are very good at picking up these social cues, almost too good. I think women hold themselves back from a lot of opportunities because they're worried about intruding, when they shouldn't be.

In networking, there are two phrases that I think people should never say: 'I'm okay' and 'I'm busy'.

If someone asks you 'How are you?' and you answer 'Okay'. Okay is boring. It's not engaging or exciting.

'I'm busy' is another terrible response (and so is 'I'm super busy'). What does busy mean? Does that mean you don't have time to take on new challenges or seize new opportunities? Does it mean you don't want to talk to me? Saying you're busy can turn people off. Busy is a response that closes doors. It makes people think you don't have time for new opportunities. We mistakenly think it shows that we're sought after and important, but the expression backfires more often than it works.

There's the old saying that if you want something done, give it to a busy person. I believe in that because there's a good momentum that builds when people are busy, they're firing on all cylinders, they're efficient, they get to the point, they get things done. I love being busy; I just don't like telling people I'm busy.

When people ask me how things are going or how I am, I just say, 'I've got exciting projects on the go right now. I'm just loving life.' That generally gets a response along the lines of: 'Wow, what are some of those projects?' If you can answer in a way that piques someone else's interest enough to ask you about it, you've got your window to showcase what you are working on and promote it without bragging.

 *The best networking happens when the relationships have mutual benefit, they are authentic, and are given time to deepen organically.*

I want to take a moment to emphasize the importance of having a strong 'personal brand'. Your personal brand is what other people say about you when you're not there. Your words and behavior (actions) will shape your brand over time. It's, something you have total control over as long as you are aware of two main things: how you want to be perceived and how others currently perceive you. Where there is a disconnect, you have work to do.

To build your personal brand you need to get noticed, showcase your abilities, build fans within your organization and expand your circle of influence.

I attended a media training course a number of years ago that offered tremendous value and I continue to use the lessons learned. The best take-away from that training session was to know your key messages and stick to them.

If a reporter called you right now and started grilling you, what would your key messages be? Always think ahead and be prepared. How do you want other people to perceive you? If they ask you something about your corporation, your business or your personal life that maybe isn't going as well, steer the conversation back to where you want it to go and get your key messages across.

That brings me back to networking: if you're at an event and you've set your goals, rehearse your key messages so that they're at the top of your head, ready to go. What are the three big things that you need to communicate to catch someone's interest for a follow up meeting? If you're prospecting, highlight up to three things that would be of interest so that they might be prompted to ask for more.

Have some standard, yet adaptable, responses handy that fit each situation. For example, when I was a financial advisor and at an event where a female executive approached me to ask what I did, I would answer 'I work with female executives to help them with the one thing they can't buy more of: time.' My thinking was that it was more likely to generate interest in me than simply stating I'm a financial advisor or a wealth manager. It prompted a follow up question to ask what I mean by that.

I could then add, 'Executives are busy doing what they do best, running their company and therefore tend to procrastinate when it comes to managing their own finances and often miss out on wealth building opportunities. I help spot the opportunities they don't have time to identify and help them to capitalize on those opportunities. I keep reviews short, succinct and effective so my clients can get back to running their business.'

Next I would try to find out more information by asking open-ended questions like:

- What do you love the most about what you do?
- What are the three things you could change if you could?
- What do you like best about working with your financial advisor?
- What services would you like to get from your financial advisor that you are not yet receiving?

They're going to tell you exactly what you need to hear and after answering you can say, 'That's great to hear because you know what? These are the three things that we do best.' and you can relate it to what their needs are.

Keep in mind, what you say must be true. Effective networking is not an exercise in saying whatever you think people want to hear.

 *Networking is about showcasing your true talents and skillset and matching them to another person's needs.*

Remember the win-win scenario I keep mentioning? If the relationship isn't a fit, you have to be honest about that too. Be selective about who you want to work with, whatever business you're in, and be prepared to let people go. Most people will respect and value your honesty and appreciate that you don't waste anyone's time trying to fit a square peg into a round hole. Focus on the win-win.

Networking brings benefits into every aspect of your life. Everybody needs connections for something, whether you're trying to lose weight, you want to learn Spanish, you're looking for a new dentist, your yard is a disaster and you're looking for a new landscaper, your house needs cleaning or you need physiotherapy. Think about all the products and services that each of us use every day. Networking allows you to connect and get referrals from other people for services that you may be looking for and it allows you to connect to other people with services that they may be looking for. It activates word of mouth.

When you're starting out, networking can be uncomfortable, but stick with it and push beyond your comfort zone. Make a commitment to attend a certain number of events every month and prepare yourself for them. Figure out what your priorities are and how to balance them in your Life Wheel. If your priority is business growth and you want to fast track it, I suggest that you attend a networking function every week. It might be a Chamber event, a fundraiser or a cocktail party.

It doesn't have to be a business event to spot business opportunities. If you attend a friend's birthday party, you may not know everyone in the room and chances are there will be friends-of-friends in attendance. They may be potential clients or they may be potential employers if you're looking for a change. You'll never know what's going to come out of it, so just get out there.

On the other hand, if I'm at a networking event and I know it's not a fit for me, I leave as soon as I can. I used to worry about being rude but. now if there is an opportunity to excuse myself, I do. My time is too valuable to burn it on wasted activities, and your time should be too.

Here's another tip. Before your network starts to grow, invest in a relationship management system—whether it's Maximizer, Outlook CRM, ACT, it doesn't matter. Pick one and learn to use it to track the people you're meeting and schedule follow-ups. If you're trying to remember it all in your head, you'll stress yourself out and potentially miss out on opportunities you worked hard to arrange.

Contact management programs are like an address book on steroids. Not only do they have everyone's name, you can schedule reminders to follow-up, schedule appointments and keep track of notes specific to each contact.

 *A good contact management system will allow you to stay on top of everything and keeps you on the ball.*

Finally, remember that networking is not about looking for friends. Many women think they have to be friends with someone they're doing business with. I prefer to separate the two. I want to be friendly with clients, not friends. If I want to hear about their personal life, I will share parts of my personal life, and we'll have a great relationship, but it is still a business relationship.

I'm not looking for someone to go to the movies or dinner with, or have get-togethers at my house or theirs; I don't have unlimited hours in a day. I see this often in business where women cross the line and build relationships into personal friendships, then get stressed out trying to keep up. I think the reason women tend to do that is they want the client to really like them.

Bottom line: we don't have time to do it all. If you go back to your Life Wheel and your life balance, how are you going to fit in all those people? You can't. You're setting yourself up for failure by setting unrealistic expectations.

MENTORSHIP

People often look at successful people and say 'Wow, they are so lucky.' Those same people have no idea how much work goes on behind the scenes to make it a reality. Think of any elite athlete and consider the number of hours they spend each and every day training to get to the level they are at. They face mental challenges, injuries and exhaustion, but they don't quit. They keep moving forward as they are driven to achieve.

There is a famous quote by Roman philosopher, Seneca: 'Luck is what happens when preparation meets opportunity.' It explains that we make our own luck. Lucky people work hard, are open to new ideas and opportunities and are prepared to take action whenever possible. Lucky people don't give up when something gets in their way. Think about that the next time you're at a networking event as your preparation will eventually connect you with the right person and opportunity.

Several years ago, I attended a conference for female financial advisors offered by my company that was designed to support and inspire women to succeed in finance. This was right up my alley! The speakers were inspirational, the break-out sessions interactive and informative and the networking was phenomenal. I intentionally sought out key individuals to introduce myself as you just never know when those connections might come in handy. It would provide me with valuable information on the culture and vision of the firm. After meeting the president, I learned that he had a very similar career path to me (only he took it several steps further). He started as an advisor, became a branch manager, continued to move up the leadership ranks to become president.

Our discussion inspired me to look to add more value to the organization and it created an opportunity for me to share my vision and passion for the industry. About eighteen months later, after a few other discussions along the way, he offered me a senior leadership position within the firm. He recognized my talent and reached out to see if I would consider a promotion. I didn't seek the opportunity, it appeared. Meanwhile, the leadership team in Canada, where I worked, fully supported me in whatever I decided. I was flattered and excited, but turned down the opportunity as I didn't want to relocate my family at that stage in my life. I revisited my Life Wheel to ensure my decision reflected what was important to me. I was open to the possibility at a later date, but just not at that moment. As a result of turning down that opportunity, I was offered a leadership position in Canada as the western regional manager, which did not require me to relocate. Eighteen months after that I stepped into the role of national director, but I continue to work from my current location.

After fighting for what I wanted early in my career, it was refreshing to finally be at a point whereby opportunities presented themselves. It was a combination of lessons learned along the way (confidence, building a personal brand, key messages), networking and mentorship that I attribute to where I am now.

Mentorship is a buzzword these days, yet many people don't truly understand what it is or how to take advantage of mentorship opportunities.

Most people I talk to understand it to be a formalized program they sign up for. This is because everywhere you turn, organizations are setting up mentorship programs. This includes universities, colleges, corporations and non-profits. People have realized that mentorship is a great way to help people learn, grow and develop, so mentorship has become institutionalized. Don't get me wrong, these programs are fantastic, but don't let the lack of a formalized program in your area prevent you from finding your own mentor.

Mentorship can be a one-time meeting with someone. It doesn't have to be an ongoing, big, formalized process.

I have never had a formalized mentor relationship in my career, but I have worked with, and taken advice from, numerous people whom I would call mentors over the years.

When I started university, I decided to take the business program and get an undergraduate degree. A fellow student and friend who was a year ahead of me in the program offered to be my mentor. He was joking, as he was only a year ahead of me, but it turned out that he did in fact have quite a bit of information to share. He introduced me to people, helped me choose the right classes, shared tips on scheduling and good study habits. He was always there when I had questions and really helped me make the most out of my time, including participation in the infamous pub crawls.

We didn't have a formal arrangement and we didn't spend a ton of time talking, but he was someone I could go to and ask questions from time to time when I had them. That was a great initial mentorship experience for me. I was able to pay it forward and help some of the students entering the program the following year.

Once I was working as a financial assistant, I attended an event where a few of the top performing investment advisers in North America sharing their stories. Each speaker had a different story and a unique business style.

There was one speaker who really grabbed my attention. His philosophy was very similar to my own and I saw how his approach could help me become a successful financial advisor. He took a personalized service approach with his clients to deliver a 'wow' experience. Although that was a learning opportunity and not a mentorship arrangement, it did create mentorship opportunities because I very quickly learned what I wanted to know, what I had yet to learn and whom I should be contacting for more information. The presentation really got the wheels turning in my head and I found myself formulating a business plan for how I would take my career to the next step.

Think of all the conferences that people attend. People go to learn and get inspired. You're pumped, you're excited, and you've got all these great ideas to bring home, but then you get back to your office and start returning a few emails and get caught up in the work you're behind on. Before you know it, all of the adrenaline you felt at the conference is gone and you can't remember what it was you were going to do. Nothing changes. You keep doing the same thing over and over again. Einstein's definition of insanity is doing the same thing over and over again and expecting different results. Don't be insane, do something different. If you're going to attend a conference, take the time to think about the one thing you're going to do differently when you get back to your desk. And do it.

Whose brain can I pick on a one-on-one basis? That's how I look at mentorship.

I've mentioned before that almost 80% of financial advisors don't make it to five years. I wanted to be one of the 20% who succeed, and I wanted to be in the top quartile of that group.

I heard about a new advisor in our Vancouver office who had experienced amazing success in his first year. He had related industry experience prior to that, but he brought in four times as much business in his first year than the industry norm.

I couldn't think of anyone better to ask for help. He had a very similar business philosophy to mine, so I had a good feeling that what worked for him would work for me as well. It's important to always be authentic to yourself, don't try to be someone you're not.

Learning from a mentor means taking suggestions and applying them to your own situation. It doesn't mean doing things that don't fit with you.

I took him for lunch. He actually ended up paying and said I could pay him back once I succeeded. I simply asked him, 'What have you done? What's working for you?' and I listened while he shared his story, his philosophy and his opinions on why he was so successful.

They were great ideas and I used most of them. I experienced similar success the following year in my business. I attribute my early success to the ideas I learned from him over that lunch and my ability to act on those ideas.

The best idea he shared was to market myself in a community that was underserviced. It was extra work as it required additional travel time, but the results were worth it.

He taught me to portray confidence even if I wasn't feeling it, meet as many people as I could, and stay on top of current trends and market conditions.

He reminded me that first impressions are important so be aware of how other might perceive me and put effort into shaping those impressions (dress for success and exude confidence).

When looking for a mentor, you should be looking for someone who is ahead of you, who's better than you. I compare it to playing sports. I like to play squash, and am an average squash player. In order to get better, I need to play with someone better than me. If I always play with someone that I beat, I'm never going to improve.

The same analogy works for business. Identify a role model, someone who has had great success and you'd like to follow their same path. Reach out and call them. If they're willing to share their ideas with you, which, by the way, most successful people are, you'll learn what you need to do differently to move ahead.

Typically it's deeply insecure people who won't share their ideas with you, and it's very rare that deeply insecure people become successful. Generally it's the successful people who are willing and able to help others. It makes them feel good too.

A good mentor is someone who has accomplished what you want to accomplish and is willing to share knowledge and experiential wisdom and insight with you.

A good mentee is someone who has specific goals, is respectful of time, and is willing to take action. Do what you said you were going to do. It's often hard work, but the rewards are worth it.

Saying what you want isn't going to make it happen, taking action will. You can't just talk the talk. You have to walk the walk.

There is no magic potion where you just meet with someone and all of a sudden your life is better. A mentor is going to guide you, but you still have to do the work and that's where most people fall short.

Connect with the right mentor

Tip 1: Find someone who will add some value and lead you in the direction you are looking to go. Reach out to them and connect. Don't make it a big formalized thing. Take them for lunch, for dinner, for coffee, for breakfast, whatever is going to work into their schedule because they're the ones volunteering their time for no obvious benefit to them.

Tip 2: Find someone out of your area or who is not a direct competitor in your area. The reason my mentor was so open about sharing his success with me is because we were in two different markets. He couldn't cover my market, and I couldn't cover his. There was more than enough business to be done in each of our markets, so he shared his ideas with me to implement on Vancouver Island. In larger national corporations, this is typically how the formalized mentorship programs work. You are often partnered up with someone in a different city.

Tip 3: Don't let your ego get in the way of success. Be open to trying new things and let others show you the way. It's better to have the questions than the answers, no matter where you sit on the professional ladder. Thinking you already know everything keeps you in stasis. There's no such thing as perfection. It's good to strive for perfection, as long as it doesn't become obsessive and negatively impact results. Perfection is an unattainable goal because even when you arrive at what you think is perfect, things change and there's something even better out there. We are never done learning and we can always improve.

Tip 4: Ensure the right fit and accountability. When you meet with a potential mentor, you have to very quickly conclude if the fit is right. If yes, take action by asking for a follow-up meeting and follow up. Be accountable to ensure results.

If you're meeting with a mentor, make sure you're prepared to do the work. It's the best way you can thank them for their time and energy.

Tip 5: Find a mentor not too far ahead of you to learn from. My first mentor was a few years older than me and a little bit ahead of me in his career. I sought his help as I felt it was realistic and within my reach. If you set your sights on a mentor who's too far ahead, it might be too big of a leap and you risk losing your momentum. There are certain steps that you need to take along the way to get to where you want to go. You can't jump to the finish line.

Tip 6: Find a mentor who is still relevant. What may have worked for someone thirty years ago might not work today. Successful people need to evolve. Technology has significantly changed how we do things and how people interact. With 'do not call' lists and 'anti-spam' legislation in effect, old techniques like cold calling and mass mailings are archaic. If your mentor recommends this approach, you may want to think about finding a new mentor right away.

Tip 7: A mentor relationship can lead to employment and business opportunities, but no mentee should expect it. If it is a good, healthy relationship, the mentee can use it as an opportunity to demonstrate their commitment, their willingness to learn, their professionalism. It really can be like a long, unofficial interview. And even if the mentor doesn't have any openings, if they're impressed by the mentee to the point they can't help talking about the mentee to other colleagues, it's going to create real opportunity. Getting a job is all about showcasing your talents to the right people.

Perfection is the enemy of progress. If we wait for it to be perfect, it will never happen.

At this stage of my career, I'm more often in the mentor's chair offering advice to those who are considering a career path in finance.

As a mentor, you reap the benefits of networking with prospective talent which can help your organization grow and assist you in achieving your goals as a business owner.

You also get to give back which everyone feels good about doing. I believe that everybody should give back in one way or another. Most successful people have received helpful advice from other people along the way. What would their life have been like if everybody shut the door in their face? The world would be a nasty place if that were the case.

People—especially the most fortunate—need to not be selfish. Everyone's busy; we get that. But being a mentor is an obligation of the highest purpose. It can be small doses once a year. It could be one-off meetings. It could be agreeing to do a one hour speed mentorship program once a year at a university.

The old saying, 'the more you give, the more you get back' is not why you do it, but it happens. What goes around comes around.

Here are a few tips for potential mentors.

Agree on the time commitment: My responsibility as a mentor is to commit some time to the relationship in a way that is pre-agreed and doable for me so that I can give 100%. I prefer to set a time limit on the relationship which allows me to help to more people. Committing to meeting a mentee once a month for thirty minutes for six months can fit into my schedule. After that, the relationship ends. However, if I find at the end of six months I still want to keep that door open, I will let them know. This may sound rigid, but it respects my time and energy while still allowing me to give back. It establishes a healthy parameter for the mentee to work within. How is a mentee ever to know what works for you if you don't tell them? It also makes for easy exits from the relationship if the boundaries aren't respected. No one can get resentful about time given or taken if the time limit is agreed to up front.

Be authentic: The relationship between mentor and mentee—even from the beginning—has to be authentic. As a mentor, you need to really want to help make a difference in somebody's life. And mentees must have a genuine desire to learn and grow and be willing to take action on the right suggestion, or suggestions that fit for them. And both parties at the outset need to be very clear about what the expectations are. What do you hope to get out of the relationship? How often will you meet? etc. It may only be once, that's fine, so maximize it!

Let go of the fear: Share your ideas with others without being afraid they might surpass you. There's enough business in the world to go around and the business world will need a generation to follow behind you who can take your place one day.

Sharing ideas with others will keep you on top of your game. By teaching others, you'll deepen your own learning and often come up with new ideas to further your own goals. It'll force you to continuously improve in order to stay competitive. It's rooted in an abundance mindset not a scarcity mindset.

I've worked with many mentees over the years – those who have been respectful and appreciative of my time and those who have not. The latter I free myself from (with no guilt because I was honest and candid about my level of commitment) and move on.

I had a recent successful experience with a mentee who reached out and said, 'Sybil, I've been impressed by your career path, your ambition. Would you have fifteen minutes to share with me? I have some specific questions I'd like to ask you as I'm very interested in the financial industry.' I said, 'You bet.' She came on time and organized. She had specific questions written down. She got through her questions and when the time was up she looked at her watch and she said, 'Thank you. That's been the fifteen minutes I asked you for. I really appreciate your time.'

I was so impressed I said, 'Did you get through all your questions? I've got another five minutes if you want to ask something else.' And she took the opportunity to ask one more. It was a very successful interaction. Based on the advice that I gave her, she walked away with an action plan and next steps. I invited her to get in touch with me again once she completed them. I expect that I will hear back from her soon.

This ambitious, respectful woman earned the right to re-engage me through her efforts and her treatment of my time. She was very smart to reach out in the way she did because I am always looking to hire talent. If she follows through on my advice and continues to demonstrate the initiative, she will likely land herself a job.

Here's the flip side. I was at a speed mentorship event where a number of college students were given fifteen-minute segments with mentors. When I asked one keener what she would like to get out of the session she replied, 'I just want to know what I can do for you.' Now, I do give her some credit. She was trying to be different by flipping the dynamic from me helping her to her helping me. But it came across as insincere and unprepared, like she didn't take the time to research who would be in the mentor's chair that day.

Asking what she could do for me suddenly put me in the position (if I were to actually tackle answering that question) of needing to be the one prepped with background research and questions about someone I had no idea was going to land at my table until she was there. Not a good strategy!

My answer was, 'I can't know if I need anything from you because you haven't told me anything about who you are or what you have to offer.' Awkward.

We carried on with the discussion and I talked about some different career options. She followed up with an email repeating the same unsuccessful question along with (and here is the very temporary moment she stepped into an actual mentee role): 'Is there anything you think I should be doing differently?'

Yes! As a matter of fact, there is. I responded candidly: 'You know, I appreciate that you're keen and you're trying to look different. But your approach is coming across as insincere and that it's just a quirky tactic to try and make yourself stand out and I don't even know what you want. My advice back to you is to consider changing your approach. What mentors and employers will want to know from you is: What are your skills? What profession are you interested in? What do you bring to the table? What are your strengths? What are your weaknesses? What do you have to offer?' I never heard back.

When the gentleman I approached early on in my career agreed to mentor me, I knew in advance of that first meeting what I wanted to know. We actually only ever had one official meeting. After that, I asked permission to call or email periodically to touch base. It was granted and I made sure I made the most of those secondary opportunities. I would limit the conversation to one specific question to respect his time and get the most out of mine. And it was only as needed for a specific question that I needed an answer to such as, 'I'm facing X obstacle. If you had the same experience, how did you navigate it?' I ensured my mentor never had to have the 'This Isn't Working Out' talk with me by being organized and specific about the direction I was looking for.

People enjoy being around, and are attracted to, positive, energetic people. If you're a positive energetic person, the mentor/mentee relationship is bound to be rewarding. When I meet with someone who's young and keen and ambitious and wanting to go places, their excitement is contagious and it gets me fired up not only about working with them, but about my own career. I leave the meeting with a spring in my step and new fire for my projects.

When I get asked to be a mentor, part of me reflects back to my first year in business, being the person asking for help. I do remember how important that is. And I remember how much it meant to me when someone said yes.

Like I said earlier, I don't have any one mentor that I've gone to on a consistent basis time and time again. I get different things from different people and that's the best way for me. I know what my skills are. I know areas that I need to improve in. I pick numerous people and take the best from each of them and apply it to me. I'm creating my own ideal mentor through a combination of people. This is why I want to give back.

 *I am very grateful for the mentors in my life as they have each contributed to where I am today.*

Mentees: Getting Started Checklist

☐ Make a list of the skills you want to work on as well as your career goals. Be open to finding more than one person to help.

☐ Start asking around. You won't know everything you want to learn before you start. Don't worry about it. One question is enough to get started. Then you could figure out who would be the best person to give you an answer. You call or write and say, 'I'm interested in this profession. I'm interested in your firm. Can you spend some time with me telling me what it's all about?' From that meeting, you may identify different areas that you need to learn more about and what your next steps should be. Rinse and repeat as you go along and your goals become more defined and what you learn opens you to possibilities that hadn't occurred to you before.

☐ Make it easy to be mentored. Show up on time, organized and ready to take action. Be respectful and courteous with your mentor's time and energy.

☐ Follow up every meeting with an acknowledgment of thanks. This does not mean shower your mentor with gifts, but send an email or card that recaps your takeaways and your plan for your next steps.

☐ Remember, the best way to thank a mentor is to apply what they have shared with you in the best way for you. At the end of the mentorship period, send a personalized, handwritten thank you note. Both during and after the relationship, use social media to celebrate the achievements of your mentor and raise community awareness about them.

☐ Update your mentor on your successes, even when the relationship has ended officially. Say, 'Hey, thanks for everything. Here's what I've done since.' That will make the mentor feel really good and it will never be too late to do it. The way you treat your mentor will have a direct impact on whether or not they decide to do it again so pay it forward. Future upstarts will thank you for it.

Mentors: Getting Started Checklist

☐ Say yes! Say yes to sharing your wisdom and knowledge in an open way. Don't enter this relationship from a place of ego. You have a lot to teach, yes, but believe me, you will also learn. Be humble, approachable and generous with your awesomeness. It will always pay you back in the end.

☐ Now that you've said yes, define the rules of engagement in a realistic way. Look at your Life Wheel—where does mentorship fit? Look at your priorities and determine how much time per week/month/year you would like to give to a mentee. Remember, it doesn't have to be time-consuming or draining. It can be a meeting once a year. It can be once a week.

☐ Be clear about what will work for you and communicate that clearly. THEN STICK TO IT. No one will respect your time if you don't first. Of course, you will find yourself in mentee situations where you truly want to give more of your time because this person is really lighting you up—

you will know it when it happens. Until then, stay within your boundaries.

- [ ] Think connections. As you get to know new talent, keep an eye on the future. Are they a fit for you? Or a colleague? A client? Reward a mentee's hard work with some of your valuable social capital.

- [ ] Encourage your peers to mentor. Highlight your successful mentor relationships and recommend a way to start, perhaps by connecting a mentee with the right peer.

Imagine what a better world we would live in if everyone helped someone else. We all have something to give and we all have something new to learn.

"Continuous effort —not strength or intelligence—is the key to unlocking our potential." Liane Cardes

OVERCOMING OBSTACLES

We all face challenges in life, but how we deal with them affects other aspects of life. Overcoming obstacles is more of a mindset than anything else. Obstacles present an opportunity to put on your creative hat to look for a work-around or alternate solution. Optimists view obstacles much differently than pessimists. Optimists see the solution/opportunity more than the problem. Pessimists see the problem/barrier more than the solution.

As soon as I identify an obstacle, I immediately think, how do I fix this? For example, if the obstacle is not having enough money to achieve your end goal, figure out a way to get the funds needed. There are many different ways to raise capital: borrow / finance, apply for grants, fundraise, use savings, sell assets. If people really want the money for something that is so important to them, and are driven by the end result, they'll usually get it.

 *When up against an obstacle or problem, ask yourself if you are willing to do what it takes?*

Imagine you were in a dire situation, life or death. Your own child is critically ill and needs a life-saving surgery that's going to cost $250,000 and you don't have the money. If you can't come up with the money, your child will suffer. What are you going to do as a parent? Is that a dire enough situation to drive you to succeed? Absolutely. Maybe you'll contact the press, engage in social media to get your story told and ask for help from friends, family and strangers. Perhaps you'll coordinate some fundraisers or get a second job. You're likely to work your ass off. And guess what? You'll do it. You'll get the money because it's important to you. Thank goodness most obstacles are not life and death situations, but you can have that same fire in your belly. Because if you do, you'll figure out a way to do what it takes to make it happen.

The biggest obstacle between dreams and reality is one tiny word: No. Actually, it is not even being told no, it is the fearful anticipation of being told no that prevents people from taking action in the first place. But our fear of this word is easier to overcome because it's something each of us has full control over. We can't change what anyone else does, but we can change our mindset to ensure we don't let our fear get in the way of our goals. Overcoming fear of the word no is critical to succeeding in business and in life.

After you encounter a 'no', the first question you have to ask yourself is why.

- Did you deliver a compelling enough ask?
- Did you pitch it as well as you could have?
- What could you have done differently?
- Were you as prepared as you should have been?
- Was your approach the right approach in that situation?

When you get that 'no', take responsibility for what was within your control, fix it, and move on.

Don't be afraid to try again, especially with the person you got the 'no' from. Ask them where you went wrong, and be ready to learn from their response. Try a different approach to see if you'll get a different result. I often hear people in business blaming somebody else for the no. If you do this you won't learn valuable persuasion skills that are needed to influence others.

What if getting that 'no' was a reasonable answer? I don't like taking no for an answer unless it makes sense. But perhaps in a particular context, I hadn't thought of things that explained why something couldn't be done. If the no is acceptable to me, I start looking at alternatives.

Several years ago, a potential prospect from Africa requested that I manage her multimillion dollar portfolio. I was excited to work with this client, but the firm I work for said I couldn't open the account. I learned that Canadian advisors do not have legal jurisdiction to do business in this context as there are major tax implications and other legal ramifications. The 'no' made sense. It was beyond my control and I accepted the 'no'.

I let go and focused my attention elsewhere.

Don't continue to fight battles you will never win. It's a waste of your time and energy. You need to know when to throw in the towel.

On the other hand, don't give up before you've even tried.

When I was first starting out in the business, I was having some success building clientele in Nanaimo, a community 90 minutes north of my home in Victoria.

My new manager told me we had to close the sub-branch I set up in Nanaimo as it was costing the firm too much. I pushed back as I knew it cost us next to nothing each year. I was the one who set it up originally and secured free office space from the bank that owned our investment firm. Annual licensing fees were minimal, as were technology costs. I was generating good income from this location and was very concerned about my ability to visit my existing clients, let alone continue to grow my business. He had been told by his boss that it was costing $40,000 per year. I estimated the cost to be a fraction of that— about $1,500 per year.

I challenged my manager to show me the costs, and if it was truly $40,000 per year I would fully support the closing of that office. He soon realized, after digging up the accurate information, that the cost was in fact only about $1,500 per year. He pushed back at his boss and supported me in keeping the office open.

The learning lesson from that experience was to not take no for an answer until I was confident that accurate information had been reviewed and considered.

When I was originally offered the role of national director, I was asked to sell my book of business and move to Toronto. I understood that managing a busy practice with several clients would negatively impact my ability to perform well in my new role as there wouldn't be enough hours in the day to do both. But I didn't want to give up direct client interaction entirely as I felt it would keep me relevant and connected to the front line— and therefore a better leader. Furthermore, in order for me to maintain a balanced life, I didn't want to relocate to Toronto.

In reviewing my business, I believed that I could easily continue dealing with twenty clients while taking on the new role. I would continue to need the services of an assistant, which would help my time management. After pitching the concept to my boss, outlining the time commitment, the service model and the many benefits of having a member of the executive team directly connected to the front line (and located on the west coast), I received the 'yes' I was looking for.

Turning a 'no' into a 'yes' is easy if you have the right reasons and can convince the other person why a yes is a benefit to them as well (or at least why a yes will not negatively impact them).

Often the biggest obstacles we face are our own self-limiting beliefs.

"Not knowing you can't do something is sometimes all it takes to do it." Ally Carter

LIMITING BELIEFS

We are most often our own worst enemy.

I can't believe the number of times that I hear people actually say negative comments out loud about themselves in social and professional settings. 'I don't know if I can do that,' 'I don't have the experience,' and 'I'm not smart enough, I'll never get that job, I'm not good enough.'

If those are the words they say out loud, I hate to think of what they are telling themselves inside their head.

We all have the power to change the way we think and the messages we send.

In order to affect change, we need to take the first step by becoming aware of what we are thinking. Our brain never shuts off, it is always thinking something. Always. We're constantly talking to ourselves inside our head, and often unconsciously. We don't pay close attention to the steady stream of our thoughts unless we purposely 'listen in'. When we tune in and listen to our self-talk, the more empowered we become to direct and change our thinking. We can become limitless as opposed to limited.

If you're sitting at your desk and you've got a million different projects on the go, and all of a sudden you're feeling overwhelmed and stressed, pause to notice what your mind is telling you: 'Oh my god, how am I going to get through all of this?' and 'This is too much.' Does any of this sound familiar? You will likely notice physical symptoms of anxiety and stress, you may feel cranky or your mood is off, your hands might shake, your head may pound—these symptoms are directly linked to what you are saying to yourself. In everyday, non-emergency situations, external forces are rarely the cause for how we are feeling, thinking and reacting.

It is tempting to blame the workload, the grumpy manager, the inefficient assistant, your kids, your partner...the list goes on, but the real culprit is us.

When we take the time to actually stop and think about what's going on in our head, we notice that our self-talk is what's creating that stress and anxiety.

I caught myself doing this recently. In 2015, when I was filming the first thirteen episodes of *The Wealthy Life* TV series in four days, I was feeling very anxious. I wanted everything to be perfect, yet didn't know what to expect or how to fully prepare as I had never done this before. There were so many little things to remember: introductions to guests, messaging for before and after commercial breaks, my key messages for each topic while ensuring the guests and I stayed within our allotted time. In the four days I would cover 13 episodes with 26 guests and 39 topics. Preparation for any one topic is enough for most. My heart was racing and my body felt like a nervous ball of energy that I couldn't calm down and it was preventing me from sleeping. Not being able to sleep properly was creating even more stress as I worried about being alert and rested for filming.

What was going on in my head to cause this feeling? I stopped to ask myself and realized I was engaging in negative self-talk. I was thinking too far in advance and creating my own worry. The little voice in my head was saying things like, 'How am I going to remember all this? I'm going to forget my key messages. We're going to have to do multiple takes, but we don't have time for that. I want to get it done in one take, I want people to think I'm amazing at this.'

As soon as I caught myself saying those things to myself, I was able to change my thinking. I started telling myself things 'You've got this. Take it one segment at a time. You know your stuff. It's going to be great. Everyone will help make it easier. It doesn't have to be perfect, in fact nothing ever is. Think of how good you'll feel once it's done.' And it changed my mood. It changed my anxiety level.

Unfortunately, this shift didn't happen until day four, the final day of filming. I had forgotten to check in with my inside voice. When we get caught up in the moment, it's hard to remember to take a deep breath and talk to ourselves.

Rather than worrying about how am I going to remember what to say, I wrote up cheat sheets to tape below the camera to prompt me. That was a game changer. That little solution helped take the pressure off and reduce my anxiety. I told myself that it was okay to make mistakes. I told myself that retakes are normal and to stop putting pressure on myself to get it perfect the first time. I figured out that when I said the same thing over and over a few times, by the third or fourth retake it flowed much more smoothly.

Instead of focusing on the negative and the potential bad takes, I changed my thinking to 'These are just practice rounds. The fourth take is going to be awesome, so embrace it.' My heart rate slowed. My confidence built. I was happy and I delivered.

The reality of it is the more relaxed I became, the less likely it was I would need to do a retake in the first place. The whole day just flowed better because I changed my thinking.

Mindset and self-limiting beliefs go hand in hand.

I like to think about visualizing success. Coaches who work with athletes do this all the time. When I take on a new project, I visualize what the results will look like and more importantly, I visualize the feeling of success, happiness and positive energy. I can actually feel it. And guess what happens? I get it done. It happens.

That doesn't mean I don't fail once in a while or fall short of what I originally set out to do, but I do realize success way more than I fail.

 *Failure is either just a learning lesson or a blessing as it wasn't meant to be.*

I used visualization to learn how to knee board which is a fun lake sport where you ride in a kneeling position on a small padded board that is towed behind a ski boat. You hold on to the rope with your hands and hold the board with your elbows to start. Once the boat starts moving, you need to pull yourself up to a kneeling position without falling off and wiping out. When you get up to an upright position, you have to let go of the rope with one hand to fasten a strap across your knees to secure yourself to the board. All this happens within a few seconds while the boat is towing you at a speed of close to twenty kilometers per hour. It takes balance and coordination. Most people fall off the board when they try it for the first time. It usually takes several tries to get the feel of it.

My friend—who had done it before—told me what to do. While she was telling me what to do, I was visualizing the feeling.

I already knew what it felt like to be towed behind the boat so that part was easy. In my head, I'm being pulled. There's going to be forward pressure. How is my body reacting? Which direction is my body going to want to fall? My core needs to be engaged to keep it upright and balanced and centered. My elbows are going to have to hold the board but I'm going to be pulled and it's going to want to take me off the board. I need to put some downward pressure on to the board. Keep centered. I'll just use my core muscles to pull my knees up to my chest to get onto the board. I was visualizing everything and how my body would feel and what my muscles would do and how they would react. I was still on the boat.

My friend demonstrated and while I was watching her, I visualized again. I pretended it was me out there. I was watching her body. I was watching how she was positioning herself, where her hands were, where her legs were, where her elbows were. I pretended in my head that I was the one on the lake feeling what she was feeling at that very moment.

Now it was my turn. I jumped in the water and positioned myself. I grabbed the rope. The boat took off. Up on my first try.

Why don't we do this in business, in our careers, in our creative endeavors, in our personal life? We need to be doing this all the time so that our dreams can become our reality.

Let's say you have a meeting with a client or an important presentation. You can visualize in advance how you want that meeting or that presentation to go. When you're in that meeting with a client, what are your lines? How are they going to react? It's hard to know how someone's going to react if you haven't met them yet, so you have to visualize different scenarios. And you can prepare for each scenario and how you might answer it. Are you going to feel confident? Or are you going to feel nervous? Human instinct is to feel nervous before you get up and give a presentation or before you meet with a new prospect. You've got to change that thinking. Nervousness is negative self-talk. That's all it is.

Before you go to that meeting, ask if and why you are nervous and listen to what your answer is. If you're honest with yourself, you're going to say things like, 'What if they don't like me?' Or 'What if they don't like what I have to say?' When you're worried about that, you'll be creating unnecessary pressure. And unnecessary pressure has the potential to backfire. Breathe to relax and refocus.

Instead, go in thinking, 'the sale would be nice but, do I want to work with this person? Do we connect? I'm going to use this meeting to find out.' If it's not the right fit, promise yourself that YOU will walk away. Not the other way around. All of a sudden you've taken all that pressure off yourself. You can relax and just be you. You just shifted the energy from an audition to a two-way interview.

 *Every interaction you have with someone can be a positive experience, even if it's negative.*

Say you meet someone and you just clash. Oil and water. Uncomfortable. Awkward. We've all been there. Even though the actual experience is icky, when you stand by your own beliefs and value systems, you can say 'no thanks' and walk away. It's a positive experience.

When you go into it thinking that 'even if it's horrible, it's still a learning opportunity', you take the pressure off yourself. 'I don't want to deal with that jerk. It even feels great just to put your foot down and not let that person ruin your day.

The mindset I want people to recognize—women especially pay attention here—is a preoccupation with making everybody else happy and forgetting that you matter too.

Women are so concerned with making everyone else happy, and they don't want to rock the boat and/or they don't want other people to be jealous. I see this every day in business with women. Yes, there are still people in the world who want to tear successful women down. That's not the crime.

The crime is when women who are, or want to be successful, downplay their success or ambition to make other people feel better. That's craziness.

 *Jealousy is not good. Jealousy is ugly. And guess what? Jealousy is not your problem. It's their problem.*

And you, even strong, successful, ambitious you, can't fix or change other people. Good thing too, because it's not your job. There's no need to parade your accomplishments in someone's face or be arrogant about it (that's a sign of insecurity) but let's embrace jealousy in others.

The reason I say embrace jealousy in others is because it means you're doing something right. Jealousy is that person's issue. You can even confront them and just say, 'Look. I'm getting some resistance from you. I'm feeling like maybe you want the same opportunities and successes that I've realized. Tell me about that. What would you like to do?' Prop them up; don't bring yourself down to their level. Try to get them to step up, don't let yourself step down.

I have personally experienced that feeling of trying to hold myself back from talking about what gets me excited because I've been around people who can't celebrate my success.

I've toned it down to try and make another person feel better about themselves. It was a waste of time in the end because guess what? That person still feels bad and I wasted time and energy on massaging an emotion that was never mine in the first place. I end up not shining. And you know what? It feels damn good to shine.

And the other thing that I've learned, is people like being around positive, optimistic, happy people. And when I tone myself down, I might be making the minority a little happier and feeling a little better about themselves because I'm not shining so bright, but I stop being what is authentic to me and everyone pays for that in the long run.

Don't focus on the lowest common denominator. Don't bring yourself to the lowest level. Accept that in life there will always be 'haters.' Try and remove them from your life if you can. If you work with people who are always negative, don't let their attitude be contagious in your work environment.

Let positive people and positive energy affect your work environment.

Both positive and negative energy are contagious. The stronger force is the one that will win. So shine and shine as bright as you can. We'll all be better for it.

Most people, the majority of people, will be fueled and inspired by your positive energy. And it will encourage them to step up to the plate. Confidence, happiness, optimism, go-getter attitude, those are positive traits and they inspire others to act.

The small percentage who aren't inspired are the naysayers. Cut them out of your life. Remember! Eliminate toxic relationships!

In most office situations there's always one negative person. The old me used to worry so much about trying to please that one negative person because I'm a people-pleaser. I'm happy. I want everyone else to feel the same way. I would work so hard and put so much energy into trying to change the one negative person. (I think part of it is because I love a challenge and I want to win.) But what I learned was that I was trying so hard to change the one negative person, it was taking valuable time and energy away from everyone else. Redirecting my focus to everyone else produced better results.

Once I recognized that, I shifted gears. I told the negative person to basically fit in, get on board or move on because I'm going to spend my energy rewarding the positive behavior that I'm seeing from everyone else. And guess what? The negative person actually became less negative and came on board because they realized they were missing out.

The negative person is fueled by attention. Remove that attention and they are suddenly at a loss and have a decision to make. Change it up or move on. Think about the kid who keeps acting out because they have figured out they get whatever they want when they do. Mom and Dad jump through hoops to appease the kid and his/her moods. When it's not our situation we can see so clearly that this doesn't work. Don't do it in your own world.

Women generally don't like to toot their own horn. Every accomplishment is followed by a qualifying statement about the challenges and struggles that we're faced and the failures or mis-steps along the way. As women, we can relate to that. People want to hear the secrets, the dark, dirty stuff. They want to know it's not always perfect.

I encourage that type of sharing because I want people to have realistic expectations and goals. People like hearing those stories because it makes them feel inspired to overcome their own challenges. If everything is always happy and rosy, people don't buy it. It's not realistic. And they're right. It's not realistic because we all face challenges. It's what you do when you face those challenges, what your mindset is, what your beliefs are, and how you talk to yourself that helps you overcome obstacles and to succeed.

If you are the type of person who is a negative self-talker and you use these obstacles as excuses, you're not going to get anywhere. Be mindful that everyone struggles with something and things aren't always as they appear.

 *The grass isn't always greener on the other side of the fence, so take care of your own lawn.*

PUT YOUR HAND UP

I recently met a woman who complained that her firm didn't actively promote women to senior leadership positions and that it felt like an old boys club. I knew that wasn't true because I was privy to information that proved otherwise. I asked her if she wanted to be in management, and she said 'hell no!' I asked her if she knew of other women that wanted to be and she couldn't answer. The firm would love to have more women step up to senior positions, but for a variety of reasons, the number of women candidates doesn't seem to be growing. Perhaps it's because many women may feel that a senior role is scary and out of their comfort zone.

If your goal in life includes a step into the C-suite, stop overthinking it and don't question your ability to do the job. Almost every job is a "learn-as-you-go" affair. The C-suite is no different. Don't let negative self-talk and get in the way of your success. You may not have all the answers, but you can find them.

A recent study[11] showed that if a position is posted and lists ten prerequisites, but the candidate only has six of the ten, a male candidate will apply but the female candidate won't.

Women are more likely to hold off until they have all the listed qualifications whereas men tend to put more value in their ability to learn as they go. If you don't have the qualifications, ask yourself how easy it is to obtain? Can you learn on the job?

---

11 Internal Research at Hewlett Packard

Step out of your comfort zone to get ahead. If you're not a bit uncomfortable, you're likely not trying hard enough.

What's the worst that can happen? If you don't succeed in the job, you'll try something else. You will have learned a few new things and have a better idea of what you really want to do.

Many successful entrepreneurs failed several times before they succeeded. Walt Disney was fired by a newspaper editor because he apparently lacked imagination and had no good ideas.[12] He went bankrupt before he created Disneyland. The key is to not view that as a failure, but as a risk that didn't pay off and a great learning experience that leads to future success.

A note to employers: changing the wording in a job posting can make a difference. By simply changing the word 'prerequisite' to 'preferred qualities', you'll reach more candidates and have a better selection of talent to choose from. Understanding that men and women are different, and having an open mind to how you as an employer can increase productivity and profitability is valuable. Awareness is the key to eliminating unconscious biases.

Now that I am in a senior leadership position, some existing biases are becoming evident. As I push for gender equality and encourage women to step up into leadership roles to improve the bottom line, some of the men are getting their noses out of joint.

---

12 http://www.incomediary.com

I've been told I should 'tone it down' as I'm pissing off some of the men. This isn't about men versus women. This is about both genders being the best they can be. There are differences between men and women, but those differences should be embraced for mutual benefit. In order to get more women into the C-suite, we need to create a culture that welcomes and supports women. In order to do that, we need to educate both men and women about the benefits.

I understand that in the process of offering special training and development opportunities for women, men are feeling left out. Those training opportunities should be offered to all. However, in the past, they were primarily only offered to men which is a contributing factor to why we only have 12-15% female advisors. We have some catching up to do. The training offered to women is not designed to be at the expense of supporting men, it's in addition to.

Ask yourself whether you think masculine or feminine when hearing the following traits:

- aggressive
- compassionate
- risk taker
- planner
- big-picture thinker
- detail-oriented

I'm guessing you think like most people do and understand some of the unconscious biases we all have.

For a woman to be considered for a leadership position, she needs to convince others that she is a big picture thinker, aggressive (without being bitchy) and results driven. We often hear that women have to work harder just to be treated equally to men. I think this is largely due to these unconscious biases.

If people don't think you can do the job, you have to go above and beyond to prove yourself. We can change the unconscious biases by getting more women to step up. Women need to do a better job at ensuring their strengths are noticed by others. Women tend to downplay their strengths yet ensure others get recognition. Men need to be aware of this and pay attention to what is really going on.

If a woman thinks of a new idea and puts it into action and the results are great, when receiving praise she will often say 'Thanks, but it was a team effort.' This is exactly the wrong thing to say! This is the moment for a person to shine—male or female—if they are the one directly responsible for the success. How about: 'Thanks, I was really excited when I saw how my idea could work. And thanks to my team who believed in it and helped me put it into action.'

 *What are your gifts and how are you going to use them to shine and to benefit others?*

Answer your own questions without reserve or hesitation. Get used to seeing the confident you even if it's just on paper or in your head for now.

Identifying your natural strengths and abilities requires some brutal honesty and self-awareness. I recommend you pick a quiet time and find a quiet place to brainstorm. What am I happy about? What am I good at? What do I not like to do? What do I want to personally work on? Rather than calling it a weakness, I prefer to call it an opportunity for improvement.

Once you know all the things that you're good at, look for the best opportunities to put those skills to use. By figuring out the things that you are good at, you can match your attributes, skills, and interests to the ideal next role for yourself.

 *We need to believe what we hear. When you're given a compliment, say thank you. But more than that, believe it.*

Generally speaking, people aren't going to tell you things if they don't mean it. 'Wow. Fantastic job on that project. You knocked it out of the park.' Believe it. Own it. Sit back and tell yourself, 'Yeah, you know what? I did a great job!'

Every once and a while, reflect on what people have said to you in support or celebration of your accomplishments and sit there until you believe it all over again. It'll make you feel good. It'll build your confidence. Let your insecurities take a back seat.

It's important to promote our strengths with purpose. I know many women who have the most amazing qualities and strengths that would make them dynamic leaders or experts in whatever their field is. The problem is, nobody else knows it.

 *It's no use having great skills if nobody knows you have those skills and can make use of them.*

Allow people to see you in action. Draw attention to the things that you do well. Let people know how great you are by shining your brightest every day. (Of course I don't mean going up to people and saying, 'Hey, look how great I am. Look at all the things that I just accomplished,' because that's going to turn people off.) During the course of your work day and your work life, there are occasions and opportunities when you'll be in conversations with the people who can directly impact your career opportunities, your income levels, your salary, your bonuses. Make sure you let critical information about your skills and successes slide into the conversation. Plan for those conversations. Rehearse those conversations. Make a plan for how you'll demonstrate your skills.

Performance reviews are a good example. They provide the perfect opportunity to highlight your skills and indicate interest in new challenges and opportunities. Come prepared to a performance review with a list of accomplishments over the recent period and a list of new goals.

Share your perspective on what you do really well and what training opportunities you seek for advancement opportunities.

My staff do their own performance reviews. It's an opportunity for them to toot their own horn and bring to my attention the great work they have done. At first they hate it, because we are innately uncomfortable celebrating who we are, but the rewards are great.

Even though I see these people working hard each and every day, I couldn't possibly know every great thing they have accomplished as I have other priorities to focus on.

It's a big mistake to assume your boss knows what you've been doing and can list off your accomplishments. It's your job to make sure what you do gets seen by the right people.

The second part of the performance review is to set new goals and be accountable for achieving those goals. Tell your superiors, 'Here are the top three things I want to get done over the next quarter, over the next six months, over the next year.'

By stating your goals, you'll receive valuable feedback to ensure you're on the right path. With the boss on your side, you'll get the support the resources you need to get that goal completed.

Now that you've put it out there, you're very likely to get it done. It will push you as you won't want to fail now that you are expected to deliver.

TALK TO YOURSELF

Confidence and happiness are correlated with positive self-talk. Pay attention to what you're telling yourself. If you are in a new city and need to find your way to a specific location, do you think to yourself, 'Oh my god, where am I going? How am I going to get there?' Or do you say, 'This is an exciting adventure! Let's go grab a map and figure it out!'

We are always talking to ourselves, whether we are aware of it or not. Our brains are always working. Ever notice it's extremely difficult to clear your mind and not think of a single thing? The brain only represents 2% of our body weight, but consumes 20% of our resting energy.[13] Bringing awareness to our thoughts can help us change the negative thoughts into positive ones, which manifests into a more confident, happy person. This is easier said than done. It takes practice, but is worth the effort as the benefits are powerful.

In order to overcome self-limiting beliefs, one must first have an awareness of one's self talk.

Acknowledging our self-limiting beliefs is the hardest step, but it's the most important step. Here's an exercise for the next time you are nervous, anxious, or stressed about a decision or a meeting, or whatever. Step one: stop what you're doing and pay attention to the deeper conversation going on in your head. What are the thoughts that are running through your head when you think about a particular situation?

Once you are aware of those negative thoughts, make a supreme effort to change it. If you're feeling overwhelmed and the last thought that went through

---

13 https://www.scientificamerican.com

your head was, 'Oh my god I can't get this all done in a day.' Change your thinking to, 'I'm going to get this done because I can. And it's going to be good enough. I'm going to give this my best and whatever happens, happens. And if I don't get through it all today, there's always tomorrow.'

Change your thinking to something more positive and hopeful. Create that positive energy and that mood and that excitement. How does your body react? Visualize it. It will help you get there. If you are about to give a presentation in front of an audience and you're feeling nervous, stop. What was the last thing that went through your head? 'What if I forget what I'm going to say? What if I stumble? What if people laugh at me? What if people don't like what I have to say?'

This is all normal, negative self-talk that people think before they go on stage. Catch yourself and change it. Think instead, 'I know this stuff. I've got to go up and be me. Not everyone may like me and that's okay. I'm going to be me and I'm going to say what I have to say. And if I stumble, oh well, everybody stumbles. Nobody's perfect. It's okay.'

You've changed your thinking. You've taken a deep breath. You're going to go up on stage and you're going to deliver a great presentation. Because everybody delivers a better presentation when they're relaxed. If you're nervous and uptight and worried about everything that can go wrong, things probably will go wrong. It's the law of attraction and I'm a big believer in the law of attraction.

 *You have the power to shift any outcome that is the result of negative thinking.*

"The most effective way to do it, is to do it." Amelia Earhart

ACCOUNTABILITY

So, you're this far into the book and you're smashing your self-limiting beliefs, identifying and celebrating your strengths, preparing to eliminate toxic relationships, balancing your Life Wheel, building networks and looking into mentorship opportunities…what is it all for? I'm glad you asked because it's time to pull it all together and get serious about goals and goal setting.

I live by the motto 'Conceive it. Believe it. Achieve it'.

Conceiving requires an open mind, free of self-limiting beliefs, to think of an idea or set a goal. It doesn't matter whether it's realistic or not. That will come later.

Believing requires a further understanding of what is involved in achieving the goal and a belief that it's possible. This often takes time to research what is involved, but the process helps build confidence. It's easy to think 'that's not possible' or 'I can't do that'. Challenge yourself to think it through further and find a way to believe it is doable. Ask yourself what is needed and who can help.

Once you believe it's possible, achievement usually follows. You don't always achieve everything you believe in, but it's almost impossible to achieve something if you don't believe it's possible.

How many goals should a woman have at any particular time?

You don't want to set so many goals that you feel overwhelmed and can't follow through, but you should have more than one goal at a time. Think about your Life Wheel and have targets in each area of your life. I prefer to have fewer goals but bigger goals. From those big goals, I work backwards as there are several little goals that need to be achieved along the way in order to achieve the big goals.

Write it down

Writing down your goals—putting pen to paper—solidifies them and makes them real. It acts as a brain dump to reduce the chance of feeling like you don't know where to start. When I have too many things swimming around in my head, I get distracted, I feel overwhelmed. As I said earlier, the brain is a great processing unit but it's a lousy storage device so don't rely on it to remember everything you have on the go. The first step in achieving a goal is writing it down.

You know you've set a big enough goal, when you're uncomfortable. If you're asking yourself, 'Is this too big' or 'is this too much?' the goal is big enough.

If you set a goal that you know without a doubt is a cake walk, you haven't challenged yourself enough. Get out of your comfort zone. You've got to take risks to get ahead. It might be reputational risk, it might be a financial risk or even an emotional risk, but you've got to get uncomfortable, at least a little bit.

When I was doing *The Wealthy Life* TV show, I first thought, 'This will be great! How hard can it be?' Once I started planning it I realized it was much more work than I thought. When I realized what I'd agreed to, I was overwhelmed as this was definitely pushing me to my limit and beyond.

I got back on track mentally by asking myself if I could do it. Yes I can. How do you eat an elephant? One bite at a time. And I kept reminding myself of that when my anxiety level was high, my heart was beating a little too fast and I had a lump in my throat.

They say what doesn't kill you makes you stronger. You don't want to push yourself to collapse or failure, but most people don't push themselves anywhere near their full potential. Push your own limits for personal growth. Get out of your own comfort zone. Once you have achieved that goal, your next push will be bigger, and once have you achieved that goal, the next will be bigger still.

In other words, you don't go from zero to marathon: you go from zero to walk; walk to jog; jog to run: 2k, 5k, 10k, half marathon, full.

Weed out the unrealistic

This requires honest attention, thoughtfulness, self-awareness, honesty, and confidence. I challenge you, don't brush off the ones too quickly that you think are unrealistic. Generally they're unrealistic because you haven't done enough homework to convince yourself that these are doable. They may seem like pie in the sky, but give them consideration anyways.

Develop an action plan

As you write down your goals, and you see how big your list is, ask yourself if any of those goals need to be adjusted. Do some of them overlap? It's amazing how many activities may overlap and achieve multiple goals at the same time. If you have a goal to exercise more and another goal to increase quality time with the family, you can do both at once by going on a family hike together.

Schedule into your calendar the activities that need to get done to carry you on your way to achieving those goals. Use the QUICK method to keep focused and efficient. As a result, you'll rarely need to review your original goal sheet again. The goals and action items are engrained in your brain. The original sheet is just the process of getting your thoughts on paper. Once you have diarized the tasks to complete, you'll move closer and closer to achieving the big goals.

Sometimes goals change. Another opportunity may arise that slightly changes your original goal, makes it better or takes you in a slightly different direction. And as long as you can answer 'yes' to the question: 'Does this still fit with what I am trying to accomplish', then shift and adapt to the new direction.

Opportunity can be misleading and result in distraction. Entrepreneurs tend to like shiny objects and may be easily distracted. 'Squirrel! What's that shiny thing over there?' Make sure you follow through and get things completed.

There's something about writing it down that commits you to action, even if you never look at that piece of paper again.

Writing your goals down not only gives them power, but helps you to see, literally see, what order or priority to give them. Some will seem to vibrate on the page, others are 'quieter' and aren't demanding immediate action. You can identify goals that overlap or are at odds with each other. You can assign a sequence to your goals and break them down into manageable parts.

For example, I was having a great conversation with my son a couple years ago when we were building our new. As a teenager, he loves skateboarding and scootering. And he said, 'Mom, I want a halfpipe. Let's build a halfpipe in our new house.' I pointed out that it would take up the entire garage where I like to park my car. I had an idea: I said, 'Well, Levi, you know, there's a park just down the street. There's room to play down there. Actually there's a lot of park land there. I wonder what it would take to get the municipality to build a skate park?'

Levi was originally deflated, as he didn't think there was a chance of getting a skate park built. I said, 'I want you to Google and do some research and find out how much it would cost to build a halfpipe and a skate park with the features you want. Then we're going to contact the municipality to find out what's involved in putting a proposal together. You'll likely need to gather neighbor support and raise some capital. You might need to fundraise to pay for part of it with the municipality kicking in the rest.'

That was our brainstorm session that converted Levi's thinking it wasn't possible into maybe it is possible.

When our thinking is challenged and we give ourselves permission to be creative and open-minded, what seemed like crazy ideas become more believable.

It's now in my son's hands to see if he wants to pursue the idea or not. At least he knows it's possible if he puts in the effort.

As you're setting your goals, the brain is automatically going to think of all the reasons why it's not going to work. Perhaps it's a defense mechanism to protect ourselves from failure. I refer to that thinking as the devil on the shoulder. Listen to the angel on the other shoulder instead. Be the optimist, not the pessimist. Being pessimistic is only good as a reality check to help you think of the things that you need to do to overcome an obstacle. As long as you look at it that way, you'll be fine. If you start believing it's not going to happen, guess what? It's not going to happen. If you start believing it's going to happen, it just might happen!

What are those obstacles and how do you need to get around them? Who do you need to talk to? What resources do you need that you don't have? What networks do you have in place that you can leverage? Have confidence in your ability to achieve your goals.

As you review your goals, eliminate anything that's truly unrealistic or not a current priority, and prioritize everything else.

You might feel excited all the time, but if you never get anything done it will erode confidence, create stress and anxiety and make you feel like a failure. Stick to your knitting and get done what you said you were going to do.

Some women are so afraid of failure that they don't set big goals in the first place. Or, they set goals but keep them like dirty secrets. Both are devastating to one's self-esteem. Follow through on what you said you were going to do. You'll succeed; you'll build your confidence.

Tell people

Set little goals at first and tell people about them. It may be something as easy as starting a new fitness routine. Suppose you make a promise that you're going to work out three days a week for the next three months. Tell your colleagues at work, tell your family, tell everybody who cares about you. By telling people, you've opened yourself up to some benevolent monitoring from your community. 'Hey, how's that workout schedule going?' You want to be able to tell them, 'It's great! I'm considering adding another day.'

Share your goals with everybody. You're more likely to get something done if you tell other people about it.

IT'S YOUR TIME TO SHINE!

Now that you understand the importance of being accountable, and have realized you have the power to achieve far more than you originally thought, it's time to make it happen.

I hope I have inspired you to set some new goals and put your hand up for what you truly want in life. Given that organizations are going out of their way to find strong female candidates for a variety of roles that have typically been reserved for men, there has never been a better time to go for it. Decide what you want, uncover what's holding you back and believe in your ability to overcome any obstacle thrown your way. Believe in yourself and others will believe in you.

 *No more excuses, you have the female edge.*

Join me in changing the status quo as together we can make a difference. What you do next will set the stage for your future. You have control over your success.

Here's a checklist to make sure you have time to think through how to achieve what you want, no matter what you decide to do with your time and energy:

☐ Are you satisfied with what you are doing—whether in your relationship or in your career. Is it what you really want, or are you settling?

☐ If you could do anything in the world without any obstacles or excuses, what would you do? Is it possible? Why or why not?

☐ Can you eliminate, or at least minimize, interactions with any toxic people in your life?

☐ Do you stand tall, look people in the eye, and speak with confidence?

☐ Do you ask for what you want? Do you at least let it be known what you want?

☐ Have you set goals? Big goals can be broken into small goals. Each time you try something new or mark something off your to-do list, you build confidence.

☐ What are you doing to push yourself? To learn? To improve? What risks are you willing to take?

☐ What are you afraid of? What is your personal self-limiting belief?

☐ Have you made sure that your goals are known inside your organization?

☐ Have you put your hand up for an opportunity?

☐ What is it that drives you? If you're not sure or it's been a while since you've asked yourself this question, it's time to uncover or re-discover the answer.

ABOUT THE AUTHOR

Sybil Verch started in the finance industry at the young age of 21. She was told she would likely fail because she was young, female and pretty.

Sybil became a successful Advisor, Branch Manager and then a Senior Vice President of the largest independent brokerage firm in North America. She won the Victoria Chamber of Commerce Business Person of the Year in 2014 and is the Executive Producer and Host of *The Wealthy Life*, a national finance talk show aimed at helping people make smarter financial decisions.

Currently working on another book, expanding her television series, and active in numerous charitable endeavours, Sybil continues to set new goals and reach new heights. She believes you can do anything you put your mind to.

Sybil is positive, optimistic and enthusiastic and believes you can accomplish whatever your heart desires.

Sybil is married to her soulmate and they have a wonderful teenage son. They enjoy staying active, giving back to the community and living a life with purpose.

www.sybilverch.com